Happy
Habits

Also available by Tal Ben-Shahar

Happy
Habits

A Happier, Healthier Life
One Minute at a Time

TAL
BEN-SHAHAR

alcove
press

Copyright © 2025 by Tal Ben-Shahar

Published in the United States by Alcove Press, an imprint of
The Quick Brown Fox & Company LLC.

Alcove Press and its logo are trademarks of
The Quick Brown Fox & Company LLC.

Library of Congress Catalog-in-Publication data available upon request.

ISBN (hardcover): 979-8-89242-358-8
ISBN (paperback): 979-8-89242-360-1
ISBN (ebook): 979-8-89242-359-5

Excerpts from *Yoga for Pain Relief* including the Magnificent Seven muscle-balancing movements by Lee Albert. Copyright © 2017 by Lee Albert. Used by permission of Lee Albert.

Cover design by Vanessa Mendozzi

Printed in the United States.

www.alcovepress.com

Alcove Press
34 West 27th St., 10th Floor
New York, NY 10001
First Edition: December 2025

The authorized representative in the EU for product safety and
compliance is eucomply OÜPärnu mnt 139b-14, 11317 Tallinn, Estonia,
hello@eucompliancepartner.com, +33757690241

10 9 8 7 6 5 4 3 2 1

To my fellow journeyers,
wherever and whenever you are

CONTENTS

INTRODUCTION

In theory, theory and practice are the same. In
practice, they are not.

—Benjamin Brewster

I believe that most self-help books are born from frustration.
Mine certainly are. *Happier*[1] was a direct descendant of my
unhappiness, while *The Pursuit of Perfect*[2] was the brainchild
of my excessive fear of failure. This book on attaining lasting
change is no exception.

The particular frustration that birthed this
book resides in the knowing-doing gap—the
disconnect that often exists between theory
and practice—that I have so often witnessed
in my own and others' life. After years of
studying psychology and philosophy, it became
clear to me that my knowledge and understanding of the good life far surpassed the
actual quality of my inner life. If I was taking
an exam about public speaking anxiety, raising happy kids, or the importance of assert-
ively expressing one's needs and wants, I would
ace the test. I had accurate, eloquent, and in

The particular frustration that birthed this book resides in the knowing-doing gap—the disconnect that often exists between theory and practice—that I have so often witnessed in my own and others' life.

most cases correct answers to just about any question related to psychology. Further, I could cite rigorous peer-reviewed research to back my assertions. However, in my day-to-day life, I experienced an acute and debilitating fear of public speaking, made and repeated many unnecessary parenting mistakes, and often avoided raising matters that were important to me because I dreaded the confrontation that might follow.

While as both a speaker and a parent I had come a long way since beginning my journey in the field of positive psychology, I knew that I could do better, a lot better. It became clear to me that the path to a happier, healthier, and more fulfilled life was not to be paved solely with additional knowledge; rather, progress depended on finding better ways to apply the knowledge I had already acquired in my daily life. How would I go about doing this, though? How could I bridge the knowing-doing gap? This book is my answer.

My objective in writing this book is to provide you with an accessible and practical method to bring about lasting change in your life. Whether you want to change something in your personal life or your professional life, whether you would like to alter a deeply rooted behavior or a long-standing attitude, you will receive a step-by-step guide that will help you bridge the knowing-doing gap one habit at a time, one minute at a time.

Realize Your Dreams

I have no doubt that, like every other person, you can think of times when you attempted to implement change and failed. Was it when you tried to establish a new exercise regime or a consistent meditation practice? Did you commit to eating more healthfully or to reading for an extra two hours each week? Perhaps it was your resolution to spend more quality time with your loved ones or to keep your voice down when next arguing with one of them. And while you surely embarked on your change journey with enthusiasm and with the best of intentions, soon after you started, your energy and focus scattered and dissipated. Odds are that, like many others, you experienced frustration, even helplessness.

Cultivating lasting change surely takes effort, but it doesn't have to be a frustrating experience that is doomed to failure.

Cultivating lasting change surely takes effort, but it doesn't have to be a frustrating experience that is doomed to failure. Once you understand the distinguishing characteristics of lasting change and learn the tools and techniques outlined in this book, you will be able to realize—to make real—your goals and objectives, your aspirations and dreams.

Three common barriers get in the way of attaining lasting change. First, it's that the change is overly ambitious, too overwhelming and therefore unlikely to stick. Second, it's that the change effort relies on unsubstantiated and detached interventions that may seem appealing but don't actually work. The third barrier to lasting change is the belief that knowing what and why we want to change is sufficient to bring about actual change. Each of the three parts of the book following this introduction provides a response, an antidote of sorts, to one of the barriers.

In the first part, I discuss MVIs—minimum viable interventions—as antidotes to change efforts that are overwhelming. MVIs divide and conquer the process of change. Specifically, MVIs are *happy habits* that are as brief as possible and as long as necessary to bring about real, significant, and lasting change. Examples of these happy habits include taking three deep breaths, writing down five things for which you are grateful, reading a quote slowly and deliberately, and vigorously climbing stairs for forty-five seconds.

The second part of the book addresses the SPIRE acronym, which captures the five elements of happiness: Spiritual Wellbeing, Physical Wellbeing, Intellectual Wellbeing, Relational Wellbeing, and Emotional Wellbeing. Under each one of the SPIRE elements, I will introduce you to four brief happy habits, each of which can significantly increase your overall happiness. The happy habits included in this part—from meditation to movement, from journaling to acts of kindness—have all been subject to rigorous scientific testing, proven to bring about real change.

The third part of the book introduces the 3 Rs of change—Reminders, Repetition, and Rituals—that can help you turn knowing into doing, commitments into habits. By reminding yourself to do something and then doing it repeatedly, you are rewiring your brain and forming a ritual. I dedicate the final chapter of the book to an action plan, providing concrete examples of how you can integrate the twenty MVIs into a given week.

Practical Theory

Kurt Lewin, one of the preeminent social psychologists of the twentieth century, noted that "there is nothing so practical as a good theory."[3] Often, however, no matter how good a theory is, it is lost in translation to practice; powerful and compelling ideas that you find in books, lectures, seminars, and workshops remain dormant, residing somewhere in the abyss between theory and practice. The three acronyms—MVIs, SPIRE, and the 3 Rs—can help you bridge the gap between knowing and doing and thereby translate interesting information into meaningful transformation.

The VIVID App: Introduction

Technology can be a powerful ally for bridging the knowing-doing gap, especially when combined with research from behavioral science and neuroscience.

That's why I created VIVID, a technological platform aimed at helping experts and organizations turn any learning experience—from an article to a book, from a lecture to a multi-day workshop—into real behavior change. The VIVID app can help you implement what you learn in the following pages, from introducing a specific habit to creating an elaborate life plan.

The VIVID plan I prepared to go along with this book is designed to help you make the process of change both enjoyable and sustainable. Instead of spending your energy figuring out how to apply what you've learned, you can focus on actually doing it.

Throughout the book you will find QR codes that will allow you to access the plan. You can, if you wish, choose to add friends or colleagues to support your journey.

PART I

Divide and Conquer Through MVIs

I

Introducing Minimum Viable Interventions

> Small change, small wonders—these are the
> currency of my endurance and ultimately
> of my life.
>
> —Barbara Kingsolver[4]

What action has contributed most to your happiness? Which tool or technique made the biggest positive difference in your life? Which change have you introduced that significantly impacted your wellbeing? These are questions I'm often asked as a teacher and student of happiness. My answer to these and related questions is that it's the bite-sized happy habits that I consistently apply—the small stuff, the brief interventions, the seemingly imperceptible changes that permeate my daily life.

I call these happy habits Minimum Viable Interventions (MVIs), a term inspired by integrating Frank Robinson's term Minimum Viable Product (MVP) taken from the business world with the idea of Positive Interventions that is central to the science of happiness. I first learned about MVP as a doctoral student in Organizational Behavior at Harvard Business School, and later came across the work on Positive Interventions as a student of Positive Psychology. The term MVI merges lessons from two worlds—the world of organization and the world of happiness—into one powerful construct.

Frank Robinson came up with the term MVP in 2001 to describe a product released by a company that, while far from being the finished article, is good enough to put on the market.[5] For the company, the MVP provides an opportunity to collect data that then contributes to the next, improved, version. The MVP must also provide some value to early adopters, or else why would they use it? Analogously, the MVI, while not the perfect intervention, is good enough, and provides real value to those who adopt it.

Positive Interventions, the second term that inspired the birth of MVI, is the overarching umbrella for all the practices, tools, and techniques that contribute to a person's overall wellbeing.[6] Examples of positive interventions include meditation, physical exercise, journaling, a gratitude letter, strengths spotting, active listening, yoga, nature immersion, and the list goes on. For a practice, tool, or technique to make it into the distinguished list of Positive Interventions, it has to be evidence based, tried and tested, measurably contributing to a person's life.

The philosophical roots of the MVI approach can be traced all the way back to the fourteenth century, long before the rise of the MVP, specifically to the work of British philosopher and theologian William of Ockham.[7] Perhaps his most important contribution is what we refer to today as Ockham's Razor, or the principle of parsimony. This is the notion that the simplest explanation is usually the best explanation, that when communicating an idea or a theory, we should strive to make it as simple as possible and as complex as necessary. When we apply Ockham's Razor to the realm of self-help or personal development, we arrive at a definition: MVIs are activities that are as brief as possible and as long as necessary to

MVIs are activities that are as brief as possible and as long as necessary to bring about real, significant, and lasting change.

bring about real, significant, and lasting change. In other words, MVIs are happy habits stripped to their essence, reduced to the smallest size where they are still having an impact.

Small Stuff, Big Difference

Paradoxically, when looking at our life as a whole, the big stuff usually makes a small difference, while the small stuff often makes a big difference. Major interventions—such as a meditation retreat, a self-help intensive, a grueling boot camp, a first or second honeymoon—tend to have a minor impact on our overall wellbeing, usually leading to a temporary spike in our happiness levels and little else.[8] In contrast, frequent microdoses of physical movement, mindful breathing, journaling, acts of kindness, or expressions of gratitude often bring about significant and lasting change.[9]

If I had a choice to either go on a ten-day meditation retreat once a year or to engage in three minutes of daily meditation each day, I would choose the latter. Even though the number of hours spent on a ten-day retreat far exceeds the cumulative time spent meditating for three minutes a day over a year, the impact of the brief intervention consistently applied would last longer. If you were given the choice to run for an hour on the weekend or to move vigorously for twenty to thirty seconds a few times a day, you would be better off choosing the short daily activities. Hours or days end up having a momentary effect, while moments add up to a momentous impact.

Hours or days end up having a momentary effect, while moments add up to a momentous impact.

A Physical Example

Taking physical activity as a case in point, a study by Japanese Professor Riku Yoshida from Niigata University of Health and

Welfare, had participants exercise their biceps by merely doing one set a day of six hand curls.[10] They did this single set five days a week over a period of four weeks. Results showed a significant increase in muscle strength. Another group of participants who did five sets of six curls one day a week—who did not spread the load across the week—experienced no increase of strength at the end of four weeks. Along similar lines, National Geographic researcher Dan Buettner, who explores the Blue Zones—the places in the world where people live the longest—strongly recommends that for a longer life we should regularly *inconvenience* ourselves.[11] By climbing the stairs rather than taking the elevator, by carrying the groceries rather than having them delivered, by getting up to change channels instead of using the remote, we are engaging in micro movements, thus mitigating the harms of a sedentary lifestyle.

From an evolutionary perspective, it makes sense that our bodies and minds need the short rather than the long interventions. In our distant past, when we lived closer to nature, we didn't pause our daily routine for an hour or two at the gym so that we could get our exercise quota. Instead, brief inserts of exercise and movement became part of our ongoing routine. Throughout this book, we will explore how short bursts of physical activity and other brief interventions have a significant impact on our physical and mental health.

Incorporating the MVIs

Some of the happy habits that I introduce in this book don't require extra time or effort, as they can be tagged on things that we're doing anyway. For example, mindfully listening to our colleagues takes no more time than mindlessly participating in a meeting; with a little practice, coming up with genuine compliments can be as effortless as generating criticism; and taking the stairs can take as much or even less time than taking the elevator (provided we don't live in a skyscraper, of course).

Lest I be misunderstood, I am not against those major interventions. If we had an unlimited amount of time and patience, then my recommendation would certainly be to engage in the big and the small stuff. The problem, though, is that time is finite, and most people don't have the bandwidth for minor and major interventions. As a result, they end up doing nothing. Why? Because they believe the only way to bring about real change is through those major interventions that they don't have time for. What they don't realize, unfortunately, is the immense power micro interventions have to create change. I am all for a ten-day or even a three-month meditation retreat—if it doesn't come at the expense of a daily practice.

Time is finite, and most people don't have the bandwidth for minor and major interventions. As a result, they end up doing nothing.

Going on a ten-day meditation retreat is great and can help, but rarely on its own. When the ten-day retreat is life-changing, it's almost always thanks to the consistent and persistent follow-up of small doses of daily meditation over an extended period of time. Those who are transformed by a weeklong self-help intensive do so thanks to new rituals they introduce into their day-to-day. And those fortunate couples who are able to successfully rekindle the flame of love in their relationship following a second honeymoon usually owe their fortune to recurring practices that they sprinkle throughout their time together.

Divide and Conquer

The reason why so many change efforts fail from the outset is because they are overly ambitious and hence overwhelming. The antidote to the paralysis that often comes from this sense of overwhelm is to divide and conquer, which is precisely what MVIs do. They lower the bar, hence making change easier and more accessible.

If I think of having to go to the gym for an hour every other day, especially if I haven't been exercising regularly, I'm unlikely to start, and even if I do start, I'm likely to give up as soon as the "no pain, no gain" reality strikes. I have met dozens of people who, following a meditation workshop, committed to meditate for twenty minutes a day, but in most cases they gave up as soon as their crazy-busy life got in the way. New Year's resolutions often include the pledge to spend a few extra hours each week with loved ones, but unfortunately, very few of us remain true to our pledge beyond the first couple of weeks.[12] Once again, life gets in the way.

What if, instead of trying for an hour in the gym, you climbed up and down your office stairs for a minute in the morning, once again after lunch, and then just before you went home? What if, in place of twenty minutes of meditation, you took three deep breaths in the morning as you woke up and once again before going to bed? And what if, rather than starting with a pledge to spend hours each week with your loved ones, you augmented what you were already doing each day with a brief but thoughtful text message to a person you care about? To introduce small changes in your life consistently is relatively easy, nowhere near as challenging as most of the change that people try—and fail—to implement.

To introduce small changes in your life consistently is relatively easy, nowhere near as challenging as most of the change that people try—and fail—to implement.

Psychologist Ellen Langer asked her students at Harvard to evaluate the intelligence of great scientists. Initially, all Langer told the students was about the achievements of the scientists.

Later, she told students about the steps that the scientists took preceding their achievements. When students had only the achievements of the scientists to go by, they evaluated the scientists as far superior to themselves and as being in another sphere that they were unlikely to ever reach. In contrast, when the scientists' achievements were broken down and introduced as the culmination of a multistep process, the students could see how they themselves could conquer similar peaks. In the words of Ellen Langer, "people can imagine themselves taking steps, while great heights seem entirely forbidden."[13]

We can easily imagine ourselves taking a minute to climb stairs or breathe deeply or write a text message. And when we imagine ourselves engaging in these activities, we are more likely to actually do them, and more likely to persist.

2

Spirals of Change

The whole universe is based on rhythms.
Everything happens in circles, in spirals.

—John Hartford[14]

The most unusual, and the most eye-opening, class I took as an undergraduate was with psychology professor Richard Hackman. For years, Hackman taught the same class on the psychology of teams, which I and many fortunate students enjoyed. In the spring semester of 1996, he announced that he was intrigued by the concept of spirals and would teach an exploratory seminar on the topic. Each week we studied spirals in a different context—from neural pathways to the rainforests, from interpersonal relationships to organizational processes. Wherever we looked, we saw spirals rather than straight lines, complex interconnected systems rather than simple linear cause-and-effect relationships.

Spirals Everywhere

Today I can trace my work on MVIs back to that class. When we realize that our world is primarily made up of spirals, we understand why MVIs play such an important role in our overall wellbeing. One small event triggers another, which then triggers another, and on and on in an upward spiral, gradually expanding the scope of its impact.

One small event triggers another, which then triggers another, and on and on in an upward spiral, gradually expanding the scope of its impact.

Here is an example of a seemingly insignificant event setting off an upward spiral that generates significant positive impact. Imagine that you come into the office in the morning and the first colleague you see says to you, "Wow, you look wonderful!" Consequently, a subtle smile appears on your face. Then the next colleague you encounter comments on how terrific you look today. You are feeling good, engaging in a number of pleasant conversations. Energized and upbeat, you do good work throughout the day. You get home in a pleasant mood and enjoy a fun evening with family and friends. What a great day!

Now imagine a different scenario where a minor negative provocation triggers a downward spiral and produces major negative consequences. You arrive in the office and the first thing a colleague says to you is, "Wow, you don't look well. Is everything okay?" Well, everything might have been okay, but it is no longer. Your posture is impacted by your colleague's concern, and the next person who sees you expresses similar sentiments. You feel worse, looking to avoid further interactions, and have little energy to get on with your work. You bring this listless mood home, and all you desire is for the day to be over.

Initiating Upward Spirals

We often refer to a positive upward spiral as a virtuous cycle, whereas we call a negative downward spiral a vicious cycle. The virtuous and vicious cycles I described in the previous section illustrate how small events can and do make a big difference. What is important to keep in mind, though, is that unlike the

Rather than being at the mercy of another person to affect our mood and subsequent actions, we can take control over our lives and generate upward spirals ourselves.

workplace scenarios I depicted, an upward or a downward spiral doesn't need to be initiated by external circumstances, such as a colleague's comment. Rather than being at the mercy of another person to affect our mood and subsequent actions, we can take control over our lives and generate upward spirals ourselves. Author Christina Baldwin wrote, "When you're stuck in a spiral, to change all aspects of the spin you only need to change one thing."[15] That one thing can be a happy habit, and it has the potential to significantly impact the trajectory of your day.

Let's look at the simple act of expressing gratitude. How is it that counting our blessings each night—spending a minute or two reflecting on the things we're grateful for—can raise our overall levels of happiness, contribute to our overall success, and impact our physical health? Simply because focusing on what is going well in our life puts us in a better mood, and we're then more likely to take positive action that will lift that mood further, and on and on in a positive upward spiral.[16] Just as a single stone can cause ripples across a pond and a single candle can light up an entire dark room, a single moment can positively impact an entire day.

Moreover, because emotions are contagious, our moods impact our social environment.[17] My good mood is likely to rub off on those I encounter, and their momentary experience of positivity may trigger additional positivity in themselves and in others, and so on in a multitude of internal and external upward spirals. Oprah Winfrey, who relentlessly champions counting our blessings, describes the upward spiral of gratitude: "I started out giving thanks for small things, and the more thankful I became, the more my bounty increased."[18]

Here's another example of the rippling effect that an MVI can generate. Let's say you're having a hard time at work, feeling deflated and unmotivated. You then introduce a brief intervention where you spend thirty to sixty seconds jumping up and down. As a result of the vigorous movement, you feel a bit more energized, get more work done, and feel better about yourself. A few more positive experiences transpire as a result of the initial MVI. By the time you get home, you are more likely to go out with friends than vegetate in front of the TV, which you would have done had your mood continued to be sour.

There is something reassuring and empowering in knowing that you have some control over your wellbeing and that with relatively brief and accessible action you can positively impact the trajectory of a moment or a day. The fact that control over your mood is at least partially internal is in and of itself a source of positivity, contributing in a significant way to your overall levels of wellbeing.[19] For example, knowing that rather than passively enduring the blues, you can actively improve your mood—by moving vigorously, taking a cold shower, writing for two minutes, or committing an act of kindness—is a source of comfort that goes beyond the actual impact of any particular intervention.

> *The fact that control over your mood is at least partially internal is in and of itself a source of positivity, contributing in a significant way to your overall levels of wellbeing.*

Kaizen

Kaizen is the Japanese word for improvement, specifically referring to the divide-and-conquer approach to change.[20] It focuses on those brief, seemingly trivial, micro activities that gradually add up and lead to significant positive impact. For example, the Kaizen approach to change can be about introducing 45 seconds of climbing stairs, committing to investing an additional minute each day in your relationship, or mindfully taking four deep breaths upon waking up. These bite-sized activities make a difference over time because they have a cumulative effect (vigorously climbing stairs for under a minute three times a day is real exercise with real benefits) and because they often trigger an upward spiral and lead to more substantial action (the one-minute intentional text you send your partner can lead to a full-on date).

Sociologist Christine Carter tells the story of how, when COVID hit, she set the ambitious goal of running a half marathon and meticulously planned her training plan. The ambitious plan turned into "a spectacular failure to exercise." To get herself to move, she set a new goal: Every morning after brushing her teeth, she would get out of her pajamas and run outside for one minute. Sometimes that was all she would do, accepting the fact that something is better than nothing. More often than not, though, that one minute became fifteen to twenty minutes. Drawing on her research as well as her personal experience, Carter says that "when we abandon our grand plans and great ambitions in favor of taking that first step, we shift. And paradoxically, it's only in that tiny shift that our grand plans and great ambitions are truly born."[21]

Introducing a small Kaizen change is not as threatening as introducing a large change, and the small change can make a big difference over time by initiating an upward spiral. Once we start doing something, inertia often takes over and we continue beyond our initial commitment. The one-minute walk can gradually lead to a twenty-minute jog a couple of months later. The passionate kiss can lead to a date, and who knows to what else. One song can

Once we start doing something, inertia often takes over and we continue beyond our initial commitment.

lead to twelve minutes of music meditation, and so on. Whether or not a particular happy habit leads to more prolonged activities, the benefit of the MVI in and of itself is cumulative and real, generating positive upward spirals in our life.

Spiraling Out of Procrastination

We find an example of how small, Kaizen change can be the genesis of significant change in the research on procrastination. Most people perceive themselves as procrastinators—who put things off, drag their feet, and unnecessarily postpone important activities. The price of procrastination is high. Not only do we fail to get important things done, we also compromise on the quality of the work that we do eventually get done. Moreover, studies show that procrastinators endure higher levels of stress, have a weaker immune system, enjoy poorer sleep quality, and given all of the above, experience lower levels of happiness. Procrastination is becoming more of a problem as screen addiction becomes more pervasive.[22]

When studying this phenomenon, psychologists identified an important difference between the mindset of those inclined to procrastinate and those who just get things done. In a nutshell, procrastinators believe that motivation must precede action. In other words, they believe that to do something, you first need to be inspired to do it, to want to do it. Those who don't procrastinate, or who procrastinate less, hold the opposite mindset. They understand that rather than motivation coming before action, it is action that ought to precede motivation. In other words, act first, just do it, and inspiration will follow. Fake it till you make it, or as social psychologist Amy Cuddy says, "Fake it until you become it."[23]

Rather than motivation coming before action, it is action that ought to precede motivation.

As an antidote to procrastination, researchers recommend the five-minute takeoff strategy.[24] This strategy is about starting to do the thing you have been putting off, no matter how little you feel like doing it. Getting yourself to take brief action in the desired direction—for instance, starting the school project, embarking on the walk, or making that first phone call to a client—generates inertia and creates an upward spiral of action. The five minutes lead to five more minutes, and subsequently to five more, and so on. I often use this technique. On days when I don't feel like writing, I turn to the five-minute takeoff for help. Usually, a few minutes after I start, I get into a rhythm and can then write for two hours or more. And if I don't get into it after five minutes, I engage in another five-minute takeoff—and another, as needed. Each five-minute takeoff is an MVI intervention.

Mel Robbins, author of *The High 5 Habit: Take Control of Your Life With One Simple Habit*, takes the idea that action ought to precede motivation even further, introducing the "Five Second Rule."[25] When there's something you want to do—be it getting out of bed in the morning or sitting down to write, going for a run or calling a client—just count from five to one, and when you get to one, just do it. I often use the Five Second Rule to help me get out of bed in the morning (especially on cold days), to get to the computer and start writing, to start my exercise routine, or to get off social media. Robbins says that "the moment you feel yourself hesitate before doing something that you know you should do, count five-four-three-two-one-GO and move towards action. If you don't move in five seconds, your mental habits take over and kill your instinct to change, innovate or step outside your comfort zone." What the Five Second Rule does is, in a very short time, initiate an upward spiral.

The Butterfly Effect

Chaos Theory teaches us that a butterfly flapping its wings on one side of the globe can cause a tornado on the other.[26] Any small event can have significant impact as it spirals up or down. Chaos Theory, which originates from research in mathematics and physics, is also relevant to the psychological domain. A small psychological intervention can change the way we see the world, and consequently the way we act—and any change in perception and action, no matter how small, can generate a much greater impact over time.

The implication of the butterfly effect is not merely that a small intervention can make a big difference but also that you don't need many interventions to enjoy deep change. As you work your way through the happy habits I introduce in Part II of the book, keep in mind that there is no need to stress over adopting all or even most of the MVIs. You certainly don't need to, immediately or even in the long term, implement all twenty MVIs that I pre-

> *The implication of the butterfly effect is not merely that a small intervention can make a big difference but also that you don't need many interventions to enjoy deep change.*

sent. Pick two today, try them out for a week or a month, and then decide whether you want to continue with those two or try two others. In the words of Jim Loehr and Tony Schwartz, "Incremental change is better than ambitious failure. Success feeds on itself."[27] When it comes to implementation, less may be more.

It is now time to flap your wings so that you can make a difference in your life and in the world.

PART 2

The Science of Happiness Through SPIRE

3

Introducing SPIRE

You do not find the happy life. You make it.

—Camilla Eyring Kimball[28]

According to Aristotle, happiness is the "most desirable of all things . . . something final and self-sufficient, and is the end of action."[29] Echoing this sentiment over two thousand years later, Helen Keller wrote that "most of us regard happiness as the proper end of all earthly enterprise."[30] This idea is by no means restricted to the West. In his book *The Art of Happiness*, the Dalai Lama proclaims, "Whether one believes in religion or not, whether one believes in this religion or that religion, the very purpose of our life is happiness, the very motion of our life is toward happiness."[31]

The fact that happiness is the ultimate end suggests that all other goals are subordinate to happiness. In our context, it implies that MVIs too are means toward the attainment of the ultimate end, that the purpose of MVIs is to increase levels of happiness. This is precisely why I refer to MVIs as happy habits, and if we are to better understand how MVIs can play their role best, we have to first understand the nature of happiness.

> *The purpose of MVIs is to increase levels of happiness.*

What Is Happiness?

Integrating the wisdom of ancient philosophers like Aristotle and Lao Tzu with the research of modern psychologists like Martin Seligman and Sonja Lyubomirsky, my colleagues and I came up with a model of happiness that comprises five core elements:

- ➤ Spiritual Wellbeing
- ➤ Physical Wellbeing
- ➤ Intellectual Wellbeing
- ➤ Relational Wellbeing
- ➤ Emotional Wellbeing

Together, the five elements make up the acronym SPIRE. They provide an accessible road map for understanding, pursuing, and attaining happiness.[32] Let's learn more about each of the SPIRE elements.

Spiritual Wellbeing: Purpose and Presence

Spiritual wellbeing is about finding purpose and meaning in our day-to-day activities and in our life as a whole. We can find purpose in religion. We can also find it in our work and our homes. A banker who considers her work a calling may experience greater spiritual wellbeing than a monk who finds his work devoid of meaning. Additionally, spiritual wellbeing is about being present, being mindful. We can experience the ordinary as extraordinary when we are focused on the here and now, when we are mindful of whatever it is that we're doing or experiencing.

A banker who considers her work a calling may experience greater spiritual wellbeing than a monk who finds his work devoid of meaning.

Physical Wellbeing: Nutrition, Exercise, Rest, and Touch

Physical wellbeing focuses on the mind-body connection and is about nutrition, exercise, rest, and touch. Physical activity in the form of exercise and movement and physical inactivity in the form of rest and recovery are both essential for a healthy body and a healthy mind. The quality and the quantity of what we eat and how we eat matter a great deal—for our physical health as well as our mental health. Too many of us today neglect our innate need for physical contact and connection. We have lost touch with touch.

Physical activity in the form of exercise and movement and physical inactivity in the form of rest and recovery are both essential for a healthy body and a healthy mind.

Intellectual Wellbeing: Curiosity and Deep Learning

Intellectual wellbeing is an oft-ignored element in our overall happiness. The first element of intellectual wellbeing is curiosity. Asking questions, exploring, learning new things is not merely associated with our quality of life, or with how happy we are; it is also linked to our quantity of life, or longevity. So while curiosity may kill the cat, it helps humans live longer. The second element of intellectual wellbeing is deep learning. Immersing ourselves in a book or playing an instrument, closely observing a work of art or nature, learning a new language, or taking up a new hobby— these can provide us with a lifelong supply of happiness.

While curiosity may kill the cat, it helps humans live longer.

Relational Wellbeing: Connection and Kindness

No person is an island, and we all need to connect and to belong.

Relational wellbeing concerns the number-one predictor of happiness: quality time we spend with people we care about and who care about us. No person is an island, and we all need to connect and to belong. Perhaps the most powerful way of cultivating connection and a sense of belonging is through kindness and generosity. When we give to others, we are potentially contributing to their wellbeing as well as to our own. Self and other are connected: when we help others, we are helping ourselves, and when we cultivate self-love, we enhance our capacity to love others.

Emotional Wellbeing: Painful and Pleasurable Emotions

Emotional wellbeing is about dealing with painful emotions and cultivating pleasurable ones. Giving ourselves permission to be human—to experience anxiety, sadness, envy, or anger—is the foundation of a full and fulfilling life. The first step toward happiness is allowing in unhappiness. Nurturing and reinforcing pleasurable emotions—from gratitude to joy, from serenity to inspiration—contributes significantly to our overall experience of wellbeing.

The first step toward happiness is allowing in unhappiness.

Interconnectedness

The key thing to remember is that all five parts of SPIRE are connected—they work together as one system.[33] This has two important takeaways that might seem to contradict each other but actually go hand in hand: First, it's important to take care of *all* the elements of SPIRE if we want to be truly happy. And second, working on *any* element of SPIRE can improve our overall happiness.

The first point means that if we ignore one element of SPIRE, we compromise our happiness, regardless of how much we invest in the other elements. For example, if we don't move our bodies or take care of our health, we'll feel the impact, no matter how much time we spend with friends or reading books. The same goes the other way: Vigorous gym workouts five times a week and daily meditations won't make up for neglecting our relationships.

The second point is about how small changes make a big difference when consistently applied. In the spirit of "good enough," which is pivotal to the philosophy behind the MVI approach, you don't need to do it all. It's perfectly fine to pick and choose from the menu offered to you based on your particular needs and preferences. If you focus on just one or two simple practices and stick with them, you'll still see real benefits.

Small changes make a big difference when consistently applied.

How, though, do you choose which interventions to focus on and which to forgo? By strategically evaluating your life as a whole through the SPIRE prism and ascertaining which practices are absolutely essential for your wellbeing and which are merely nice to have.

For example, if your work requires you to move constantly—because you climb up and down stairs throughout the day or because you carry things from one place to another—then introducing additional movement each hour or two may not be necessary. Similarly, if you are enrolled in an academic course, you probably don't need to add intellectual MVIs on a daily basis. And if you regularly participate in a few yoga classes each week, the added value of extra meditation and stretching sessions may be relatively small.

In contrast, if you are deskbound most of the day, adding happy habits that move you can make a big difference in your life; if your day-to-day routine doesn't afford you new learnings, small doses of intellectual stimulation are eminently valuable; and if you are constantly distracted and engage in multitasking, a few islands of sanity in the form of mini meditations can significantly contribute to your mental and physical health.

Research and Mesearch

Each of the next five chapters includes four interventions relating to one of the SPIRE elements. All the MVIs that I recommend are evidence based and rely on a great deal of research. The research, however, cannot in and of itself tell you which happy habits you ought to introduce into your life. Research by and large provides us with general truths about the collective; it does not generate precise prescriptions that are unique to an individual. To decide which happy habits are right for you, study the research and then engage in *research*— look inside, explore your personal needs, and experiment.

To decide which happy habits are right for you, study the research and then engage in research— *look inside, explore your personal needs, and experiment.*

There is no one-size-fits-all when it comes to bringing about lasting change. Beyond experimenting with the MVIs in this book, come up with your own happy habits and learn from what others may be doing. In her article "17 One-Minute Habits That Will Change Your Life," holistic health coach Josie Santi recommends some happy habits that I have not included in this book and that may work for you—such as making your bed, fixing your posture, and adding leafy greens to your meal.[34] Writer Darshak Rana suggests not picking up the phone as soon as you open your eyes in the morning, which is what so many people do. Instead, says Rana, choose to spend the first minute purposefully, doing something that works for you: "It'll set the tone for the rest of the day and help you be more productive, positive, and mindful."[35]

The key is to continue to engage in mesearch, whether its focus is which happy habits you try on or the time of day you set aside for each of them. Let's get to work!

The VIVID App: Mesearch

While the full VIVID plan my colleagues and I have created for you includes MVIs suggested in this book, the key is to make the plan your own. Keep the practices you enjoy, let go of the ones that don't resonate, adjust the timing and frequency of your reminders, and shape the plan to fit your unique needs and lifestyle.

As you read ahead, you'll find a QR code at the end of each chapter linking directly to the relevant exercise in VIVID. If you've already scanned the QR code at the beginning of the book, you won't need to scan the codes again, as all of the practices are waiting for you in the plan. You can, however, scan the QR codes at the end of each chapter to be taken directly to the specific practices discussed in that chapter.

4

Spiritual Wellbeing MVIs

> The golden moments in the stream of life rush
> past us and we see nothing but sand; the angels
> come to visit us, and we only know them when
> they are gone.
>
> —Mary Ann Evans[36]

Spiritual wellbeing is about purpose and presence, about finding meaning and being mindful. The four happy habits described in this chapter are:

➤ Meaning in Life
➤ Strengths
➤ Mindfulness Meditation
➤ Informal Meditation

Meaning in Life

Viktor Frankl, author of *Man's Search for Meaning*, distinguishes between "the meaning of life" and "the meaning in life."[37] The meaning of life might encompass questions like *Why am I here?* and *What is the purpose of life?* Many people seek answers to these questions in religion, or perhaps in a noble mission for the greater good, such as overcoming poverty or ending global warming. While it may be very difficult to find the meaning of life, it is somewhat easier to find the meaning in life—in the ordinary things we're doing each day.

We usually have a choice in how we perceive our work—whether we see it as a job, as a career, or as a calling.

Research by Amy Wrzesniewski and Jane Dutton shows that we usually have a choice in how we perceive our work—whether we see it as a job, as a career, or as a calling.[38] A *job* is something you do because you must and have little choice about doing it. What you look forward to when you're in a job is the end of the workday, the end of the week, the vacation, or even retirement. A *career* is about getting ahead and climbing the organizational ladder. What you look forward to when you're in a career is the raise, the bonus, the promotion. A *calling* is about experiencing your work as meaningful, purposeful. When you experience your work as a calling, you look forward to more work because you genuinely care about it, enjoy it, and have a passion for doing it beyond a sense of duty or the need for a paycheck.

People doing the exact same work can perceive what they're doing in very different ways. There are janitors working in hospitals, for example, who see their work as a job, while others working in the same hospitals see their work as a career or a calling. In those very same hospitals, some medical doctors and nurses see their work as a job, while others doing the same work in the same hospitals experience their work as a career or as a

People doing the exact same work can perceive what they're doing in very different ways.

calling. Hairdressers, teachers, engineers, managers, and even parents display similar patterns. Not surprisingly, those who see their work as merely a job are less happy and less satisfied with their life than their colleagues who view what they do as a calling.

A simple change in focus can make all the difference in terms of how we perceive what we do. As Wrzesniewski and Dutton point out, "Even in the most restricted and routine jobs employees can exert some influence on what is the essence of their work."[39] Along similar lines, by slightly changing or broadening your focus, you can exert some influence on the essence of your life.

Exercise: Find Meaning

Take a minute or two to respond to this question in writing: *What do I find meaningful in what I'm already doing?*

Reflect on what matters to you in your daily activities, on what is making a difference in your life or in the lives of others. The answer doesn't have to be grandiose or major. Whether you start your day with this question or introduce it when you take a short break during the day, identifying a modest sense of purpose in what you're doing can energize, motivate, and inspire.

Strengths

Most people, most of the time, fail to use their strengths. Research done by the Gallup organization asked over a million people around the world the following question: *Which do you think will help you improve the most: knowing your strengths or knowing your weaknesses?* The majority of people, regardless of their country of origin, said it was more important to focus on their weaknesses. Interestingly, those who answered that it was more important to focus on their strengths were disproportionately more successful as well as happier.[40] Martin Seligman, Christopher Peterson, and others extended this correlation and demonstrated a causal relationship—showing that teaching people to focus on their strengths contributes to their success and wellbeing.[41]

Teaching people to focus on their strengths contributes to their success and wellbeing.

Peter Drucker, one of the most important management and leadership experts of the twentieth century, wrote that to perform at our best, we must operate from our strengths rather than from our weaknesses: "It takes far more energy to improve from incompetence to mediocrity than to improve from first-rate performance to excellence."[42] To be at our best, we need to focus on and invest in our strengths. This is not to say that we should neglect or ignore our weaknesses, but rather that we shouldn't neglect or ignore our strengths.

To identify your strengths, find the overlap between your performance strengths and your passion strengths.[43] Performance strengths relate to your talents, to those areas where you have the most potential. To identify performance strengths, simply ask, *What are my strengths?* or *What am I good at?* Is it that you can pick up a new language with relative ease? Is it mathematics? Is it your empathy and ability to really listen to someone? Are you a gifted writer or athlete? As the name suggests, performance strengths are about performance—meaning they're about the skills and abilities where you see real progress or identify significant potential for improvement.

To identify your strengths, find the overlap between your performance strengths and your passion strengths.

Passion strengths are primarily about those things that strengthen you, that fuel you. The questions to ask for identifying your passion strengths are *What gives me strength?* and *What energizes me?* For example, does sitting down and thinking about a strategy for your team energize you? Are you fueled each time you participate in large group meetings, or do you feel invigorated when you spend one-on-one time with someone? Are you passionate about working with numbers and solving equations? Different people enjoy different activities. One person's hell may be another's heaven.

Once you discover your performance and passion strengths, the key is to identify the overlap between the two. It is at the overlap where your peak potential zone resides, where you enjoy peak experience (happiness) and peak performance (success).[44] While it's impossible to spend all or even most of our time in this zone, the more time we spend there, the happier and more successful we'll be.

Exercise: Identify Your Strengths

Take a minute or two to respond to the following two questions:

1. What are my strengths? In other words, identify what it is that you're good at.
2. What gives me strength? In other words, identify what it is that you're passionate about.

After answering these two questions, pinpoint the overlap between your responses. Pick one strength that resides in the overlap between your passion and performance strengths. Commit to using this strength in activities that you are already engaging in throughout the day or week.

Mindfulness Meditation

Mindfulness meditation is about present-moment awareness, about being in the here and now.[45] This is a very broad definition that encompasses a vast array of practices. Perhaps the best-known and most common form of mindfulness meditation entails sitting down or lying down while focusing on the breath going in and out. That is, however, by no means the only form of practice. Walking and focusing on the sensations you experience as you take each step is a popular form of meditation, as is lying down and scanning your body. Praying with intention, focusing on the words and their meaning, is a form of meditation. Listening to music, not as background but in the foreground, is meditating, with all the benefits thereof.

Mindfulness meditation is about present-moment awareness, about being in the here and now.

There are numerous benefits to establishing a formal meditation practice. In various studies conducted by Jon Kabat-Zinn, Richard Davidson, Sara Lazar, and others, meditation was shown to positively impact cognitive function (improving attention, memory, and creativity), physical health (strengthening the immune system and lowering inflammation), and mental health (reducing anxiety, anger, and depression).[46] While these benefits result from meditating for twenty minutes each time or, better yet, an hour, much-shorter sessions can be extremely effective. UCLA professor Daniel Siegel recommends meditating for three minutes a day, claiming that "the brain responds to repetition with more gusto than it does to duration."[47]

Spending a minute focusing on the air going in and out of your nostrils, or observing your belly rise as you inhale and drop as you exhale, goes a long way. Another mindfulness meditation practice, ideal as an MVI, is about scanning

Spending a minute focusing on the air going in and out of your nostrils, or observing your belly rise as you inhale and drop as you exhale, goes a long way.

a part of the body that is particularly tense—forehead, shoulders, chest, or belly—and then relaxing that part, breathing out any tension that has accumulated there. A minute of this kind of mindful relaxation can go a long way toward bringing more serenity to your life as a whole.

A widely researched form of meditation that has proven to be useful for both success and happiness is visualization.[48] Take a minute to visualize a desired outcome, be it successful completion of a task, a confident interaction, or a healthy lifestyle. LeBron James, one of the greatest basketball players of all time, takes a brief moment before every game to visualize himself performing on the court.[49] James recognizes that cultivating healthy mental habits is just as critical as cultivating physical ones for peak performance.

Exercise: Meditate

Take anywhere between a minute and three minutes to meditate on your breath, on the air going in and out through your nose, or on your belly rising and falling.

You can lie down, sit down, or stand up while you breathe slowly and gently. You can focus on the sensation in your nostrils, on your belly, or on the movement of the air through your body. If you prefer other forms of meditation—such as listening to music, praying, walking, or scanning your body—then by all means engage in those. Feel free to stick to one type of meditation or to experiment with many. Start your day with a brief meditation, and then incorporate brief sessions during lunchtime, before you go to bed, or whenever you feel in need of a precious present.

Informal Meditation

Meditation can be practiced formally or informally. Mindfulness meditation, described in the previous section, is formal—it is about setting time aside that is dedicated to present-moment awareness. Informal meditation is about being present while carrying out an activity whose primary purpose is something other than meditation—be it writing a book, playing with a pet, working on an spreadsheet, or listening to a friend.

We can be mindful anywhere and anytime—right now of the words we're reading or the breath we're taking, or while participating in a meeting or doing laundry. In the words of Dr. Elisha Goldstein, author of *The Now Effect*, "mindfulness is basically just being aware, and can be practiced both informally and formally . . . When you're practicing it informally, that means that you're simply attempting to be more aware in everything that you do—and that mentality can be infused into pretty much anything. But the formal practice of mindfulness is mindfulness meditation."[50] You will derive the benefits of meditation—for your physical and mental health—whether you do it formally or informally.

> *We can be mindful anywhere and anytime*

The distinction between the informal and the formal practices, between simply being mindful and mindfulness meditation, is similar to the distinction between informal and formal exercise. Informal exercise occurs when you exert energy as you go about your everyday activities, such as while walking to work, cleaning the house, carrying groceries, or playing with your dog. These are things you do as you go through your day that count as exercise and contribute to your fitness. Formal exercise involves putting time aside to go to the gym or to go for a run in the park. Informal meditation is about bringing presence to whatever it is that you do, whereas mindfulness meditation, the formal practice of mindfulness, is like taking your mind to the gym.

When we're present, no matter what we're doing, we elevate the ordinary to the extraordinary. By becoming mindful of whatever it is that we're doing as we're doing it, any experience—literally any experience—can become a spiritual one. Vietnamese Buddhist monk Thich Nhat Hanh noted that "at any moment, you have a choice, that either leads you closer to your spirit or further away from it."[51]

When we're present, no matter what we're doing, we elevate the ordinary to the extraordinary.

Exercise: Meditate Informally

Throughout the day, return your focus to the present moment. Create reminders to help you return to the here and now regardless of what you're doing at the moment. Reminders can take various shapes and forms. You can set your smartphone to ping you regularly or randomly throughout the day. You can also put the word *NOW* on your screen saver or a picture of a person meditating on your wall to prompt you to return to the present. After a while, with some initial help from the reminders, you will find yourself returning to the present unprompted and with much joy.

The four spiritual MVIs in this chapter—meaning in life, strengths, mindfulness meditation, and informal meditation—provide a mere glimpse into how small changes can contribute to our overall sense of purpose in life and to how present we are in our day-to-day activities. There are many additional happy habits that can contribute to our spiritual wellbeing.

For example, nature is an inexhaustible source of spiritual experiences—a short walk in the woods, a brief time-out in front of the ocean, looking up at the sky, or a minute to literally smell the flowers. Reading a religious or an otherwise inspiring text can bring us closer to our spirit, as can singing, chanting, or listening to music that moves us.

In the next chapter we focus on the second element of SPIRE, physical wellbeing, and explore how minor practices can have a major impact on our health and happiness.

The VIVID App: Spiritual Wellbeing Plan

Scan the QR code below for the spiritual wellbeing exercises. If you've already scanned the QR code at the beginning of the book and received access to the full plan, there's no need to scan the code again, unless you would like to be taken directly to the specific exercises described above.

5

Physical Wellbeing MVIs

There's no better day than today to start making
those healthy changes. You can start small.

—Michelle Obama[52]

Physical wellbeing focuses on the mind-body connection and
the importance of nutrition, exercise, sleep, and touch on our
psychological and physiological health. The four happy habits
described in this chapter are:

> ➤ High-Intensity Bursts
> ➤ Strengthen and Stretch
> ➤ Cold Showers
> ➤ Breathing

High-Intensity Bursts

Movement is essential to our wellbeing. In a study conducted at
the University of Cambridge, participants were pinged on their
smartphones and asked how active they had been over the past
fifteen minutes. Researchers found that those who had moved
in the previous quarter of an hour were happier than those who
had been in a chair or lying down. Moreover, movement in
general was associated with overall life satisfaction.[53]

It is also a well-established and well-known fact that beyond its benefits to our physical health, aerobic exercise contributes significantly to our mental health—helping us deal with anxiety, depression, and other mental health conditions.[54] More-recent research points to the value of High-Intensity Interval Training (HIIT) and High-Intensity Circuit Training (HICT).[55] This form of exercise involves high-intensity movement for a brief period, followed by a break to allow recovery, then another burst of movement, and then a break again, and so on. HIIT and HICT are highly efficient, generating significant health benefits in a short time.[56]

Research points to the value of High-Intensity Interval Training (HIIT) and High-Intensity Circuit Training (HICT).

Various studies demonstrate that we don't need to do it all at once and can spread the sets throughout the day. The effect of high-intensity bursts remains strong even if there are substantial breaks between the sets. In a study based on the Wingate Anaerobic Test, participants engaged in three high-intensity bursts during the day with four hours separating each session. After doing this every other day for eight weeks, their peak oxygen uptake, a measure of their aerobic capacity, increased by 14 percent.[57] With this and similar studies showing the cumulative impact of isolated high-intensity bursts, the excuse that we don't have enough time to exercise is no longer valid. All we need is a minute here and there to meet the daily or weekly recommended amount of exercise.

If you're over forty or have any medical issue, it is important that you see your doctor before implementing a HIIT regime. And if your doctor doesn't recommend HIIT, then you can implement LIIT—Low-Intensity Interval Training—by walking or climbing stairs for a minute every couple of hours or moving your hands up, down, and sideways a few times a day.

More and more medical doctors are suggesting that "sitting is the new smoking."

It's not just happiness that's affected by movement. More and more medical doctors are suggesting that "sitting is the new smoking." We are more likely to develop chronic disease if we spend hours each day without movement.[58]

Putting all the above research together, it would prove extremely valuable to sprinkle very brief twenty- to forty-second bouts of high-intensity movement throughout the day. You can sprint on the spot, engage in jumping jacks, or skip rope; do push-ups, pull-ups, or planks; or perform lunges, burpees, or any activity that will get your heart racing. Needless to say, moderate the pace and the difficulty level of each exercise based on your fitness level and age. This is not a race, and there is nothing that you need to prove. You don't need to go all out to gain the many benefits of a high-intensity burst.

It may be wise to start with low-level intensity exercises in the morning as your body warms up, gradually build up to higher levels of intensity throughout the day, and then slow down as the day comes to an end and your body is getting ready for shutdown. You get a solid workout with remarkable benefits to both your body and mind by doing different exercises throughout the day.

Exercise: Move it!

Every two or three hours, engage in twenty to forty seconds of exercise appropriate to your age and fitness level. Ideally, work on a different muscle group each time you engage in the exercise.

Decide in advance on a daily or even weekly sequence of diverse high-intensity exercises that engage both your lower and upper body. As you get closer to your bedtime, reduce the intensity of your exercise so that it doesn't interfere with your sleep. The movement doesn't need to be overly demanding. It is better to err on the side of too easy than too hard. A bit of discomfort rather than extreme discomfort is the way to go.

Strengthen and Stretch

One of the consequences of the sedentary lifestyle most of us live today is that our muscles become tight and weak and hence more prone to injury. We are also more likely to experience pain and compromised mobility. Sitting in front of a computer for hours each day leads to shorter muscles and to muscle atrophy—to loss of flexibility as well as decreased strength.[59] Given the mind-body connection, these consequences of a sedentary lifestyle exact a hefty psychological price.

Sitting in front of a computer for hours each day leads to shorter muscles and to muscle atrophy—to loss of flexibility as well as decreased strength.

An effective antidote to our chronic inactivity, beyond movement, is combining strength training with stretching. Lee Albert, the founder of Integrated Positional Therapy, points out that the root of most injuries and physical pain is an imbalance in our musculoskeletal system.[60] For example, given that most of us are slouched in our seats for so many hours a day, our upper back muscles are long and our chest muscles are short. This imbalance is a cause of neck and back problems. Another common imbalance exists in the arm. Because we type and grab things, our rear forearm muscles tend to be long while the front muscles of our forearm tend to be short. This imbalance is a major cause of carpal tunnel syndrome, tennis elbow, and golfer's elbow.

The key to overcoming imbalance and the resulting pain is to stretch (hence lengthen) muscles that are too short and strengthen (and thereby shorten) muscles that are too long. In most people, given our modern lifestyle, the front muscles of the body are too short while the rear muscles are too long. The only exceptions are the muscles of our lower leg, where the shin (front) muscles are usually long and the calves (rear) are short.

Lee Albert's prescription is to spend at least a minute at a time lengthening each of the major muscle groups that are short (front of body plus calves) and then spend thirty to sixty seconds at a time strengthening the major muscle groups that are long (back of body plus shins). Personally, after suffering from lower back and hip pain for years, I can attest that incorporating a few minutes a day of Lee Albert's "Magnificent Seven" protocol made the discomfort go away. And there are many like me whose lives were changed for the better as a result of a few simple exercises. Medical doctor Clifford Schilke asserts that Integrated Positional Therapy "should be taught to every medical student, and should become an important component of the practice of every primary care physician and every other medical specialist concerned with acute or chronic pain."[61]

According to Albert, stretching must be gentle and should not hurt. It is far better and safer to understretch than it is to overstretch. When it comes to strengthening the muscles, it is better to lift too little rather than too much (unless you're training for a bodybuilding competition, in which case the *no pain, no gain* maxim makes sense). Most importantly, listen to your body.

A few minutes a day can quite literally change your life for the better. And if, especially while stretching, you focus on the tension in your muscles, you are adding the benefit of mindfulness meditation—getting two happy habits for the price of one!

Exercise: Lee Albert's Magnificent Seven

Spend a minute or so on each of the seven exercises below. You can do them all at once (ten to fifteen minutes) or spread them throughout the day. For a more elaborate, visual guide, with different options for each of the stretches, see Appendix B at the back of the book.

1. Stretch your wrist flexors. Push your palms together while holding your fingers spread.
2. Stretch your quads. Sit on your heels or bring your ankle toward your seat muscles.
3. Stretch your chest. Open your chest and contract your upper back muscles.
4. Strengthen the backside of your body. Lying on your back, feet flat, lift your hips up.
6. Stretch your calves. Do a downward dog with your knees bent.
5. Stretch your psoas. Standing with your front leg bent and your back leg straight, push your hip and chest forward.
7. Stretch the outside of your thigh and piriformis. Sitting down, bend one leg over the other and turn your body.

Cold Shower

It is probably the case that for most people, taking a cold shower is the least pleasant of all the MVIs. It is also probably the case that for most people, taking a cold shower is among the most beneficial happy habits.[62]

Research by Geert Buijze from the Academic Medical Center in Amsterdam points to the impact of cold showers on our

> *It is also probably the case that for most people, taking a cold shower is among the most beneficial happy habits.*

immune system—we're less likely to get sick and more likely to bounce back promptly when we are unwell.[63] A cold shower speeds up the body's metabolism, which leads to higher energy levels and increased alertness. Following vigorous exercise, a cold shower can help reduce physical pain and promote faster recovery of the muscles. There is even some evidence suggesting that regular cold showers can help alleviate symptoms of depression and anxiety.[64]

Taking a cold shower doesn't mean giving up on the pampering pleasure of a hot shower or bath. Personally, I love showering with warm water and initially experienced the cold water at the end as punishment following a treat. Today, however, having persisted for the past couple of years, I usually (though not always) look forward to the cold part of the shower and even crave it. And I always feel better—physically and psychologically—after the cold immersion.

Taking a cold shower doesn't mean giving up on the pampering pleasure of a hot shower or bath.

How cold should you go? That is still up for debate. Some research shows that even going below sixty degrees Fahrenheit (fifteen Celsius) can do the job, though it is of course possible to get a lot closer to the freezing point. Many people, myself included, find extremely cold water invigorating.

There are various other ways of getting the benefits of cold water. On the least intrusive extreme, washing your face or extremities with cold water can wake you up and energize you. On the other extreme, sitting in an ice bath or immersing yourself in very cold water outside can bring about numerous physical and psychological benefits. Choosing to enter very cold water outdoors—whether a pond or an ocean—needs to be done with supervision, of course. And if you have a heart condition, consult your doctor before subjecting your system to any low-temperature immersion, even if it's merely thirty seconds under a cold shower.[65]

Exercise: Take a Cold Shower

Each time you take a shower, end it with at least thirty seconds under the cold water. You can gradually build up to a minute or two, but you certainly don't have to and thirty seconds is good enough.

You may prefer to lower the temperature gradually so your body gets used to the cold, or it may be easier to switch from hot to cold rapidly and, rather than contemplating what and how you should proceed, just do it.

Breathing

One of the most powerful happy habits is, quite literally, right under your nose. And yet, despite the ubiquity and accessibility of the breath, it is underutilized. By learning to control your breath and to engage in different types of breathing, you can gain control over your nervous system and use it to excite or to relax, to raise energy levels or to induce calm. How does your breath modulate the nervous system? In general, slow breathing relaxes and rapid breathing stimulates. Additionally, the ratio between your inhale and your exhale matters in that a longer inhale triggers the sympathetic system, which is responsible for increasing arousal levels, while a longer exhale activates the parasympathetic system, which is responsible for decreasing levels of arousal.[66]

In general, slow breathing relaxes and rapid breathing stimulates.

A few types of breath can, in as little as thirty to sixty seconds, help you focus better, calm you down, improve your mood, or energize you. In our crazy-busy lives, these MVIs provide vital *islands of sanity*. Here are a few examples of breathing techniques that can help.

The first technique is simply about breathing slowly, gently, quietly, and mindfully. Even a minute of this kind of breathing—effortlessly inhaling and exhaling through the nose, allowing the belly to rise and drop—can help you shift from the fight-or-flight stress response to what Harvard professor Herbert Benson calls the relaxation response.[67]

Another popular technique is *coherent breathing*, which involves inhaling through your nose for five to six seconds and then exhaling for the same amount of time.[68] A minute of coherent breathing is a great antidote to both anxiety and fatigue, helping us find both calm and alertness. Five to twenty minutes daily of this form of breathing is great, but even a minute twice a day can go a long way.

Another form of breathing that has become quite popular is the four-seven-eight sequence, where you breathe in through your nose for a count of four, then hold your breath for a count of seven, and finally exhale for a count of eight.[69] As long as the ratio remains the same, the length of the parts of the practice can fluctuate. This means that you may vary the speed of each part by altering how quickly or slowly you count. While the recommendation is to inhale through your nose, you may choose to exhale through your mouth or nose.

Other breathing techniques that I recommend experimenting with for a minute at a time are box breathing (inhale for four, hold for four, exhale for four, and then hold for four); the physiological sigh (inhale all the way to the top through your nose, inhale further, and then exhale slowly);[70] and alternate nose breathing (inhale and then exhale through your right nostril as you close your left nostril, and then inhale and exhale through your left nostril as you close your right nostril).[71] Experiment with these breathing techniques, and then pick those that work best for you. Scattering one-minute breathing practices throughout your day can quite literally transform your overall experience, helping you to find greater calm and alertness, better mood and better health.

Scattering one-minute breathing practices throughout your day can quite literally transform your overall experience, helping you to find greater calm and alertness, better mood and better health.

Exercise: Breathe!

Set a reminder on your phone or calendar to pause for a minute to practice breathwork three or four times a day. Your morning routine could include coherent breathing to help you focus as you start your day. Then toward the end of the day, you could engage in a technique that emphasizes a longer exhale, such as the four-seven-eight sequence, to relax you further.

Throughout the day, either at fixed times or whenever the need arises, introduce one of the breathing techniques. Experiment with the different techniques I've mentioned above as well as others to find the right fit for you.

The four happy habits in this chapter—High-Intensity Bursts, Strengthen and Stretch, Cold Showers, Breathing—are just a few of many practices that can contribute to our health and happiness. Additional physical MVIs can focus on different aspects of health. For example, to improve your nutrition you can commit to drinking a cup of water when you wake up and then at different times during the day, or eating a fruit or vegetable at a particular time. To relax your body, you can lie on the floor with your legs up for a couple of minutes or massage your hands for thirty seconds. And to capitalize on the mind-body connection, in order to feel more confident, you can sit or stand in a power pose for thirty seconds with your shoulders back and head up high.[72]

We now shift our focus from the physical to the intellectual and in the next chapter explore how our thoughts impact our happiness.

The VIVID App: Physical Wellbeing Plan

You can scan this QR code to directly access the exercises from this chapter.

6

Intellectual Wellbeing MVIs

The wisdom of the wise, and the experience of
the ages, may be preserved by quotation.

—Isaac Disraeli[73]

Intellectual wellbeing is about being curious, asking questions, and being open to experiences. It is also about learning through books, art, and nature. The four happy habits described in this chapter are:

> ➤ Words, Quotes, and Excerpts
> ➤ Appreciative Questions
> ➤ Journaling
> ➤ Curiosity

Words, Quotes, and Excerpts

Words create worlds; concepts conceive. The words that we think about and use shape our lives and the lives of those around us. Andrew Newberg, director of research at the Myrna Brind Center of Integrative Medicine, and Mark Waldman from Loyola Marymount University write in their book *Words Can Change Your Brain* that "a single word has

*Words create
worlds;
concepts conceive.*

the power to influence the expression of genes that regulate physical and emotional stress."[74] They point to research showing that "the longer you concentrate on positive words, the more you begin to affect other areas of the brain. Functions in the parietal lobe start to change, which changes your perception of yourself and the people you interact with."[75]

We are exposed to words—negative, positive, and neutral— constantly. Within one paragraph in the daily paper or in a timeless novel, we are often taken from the exhilarating heights of Olympus to the depressing depths of Hades. And while all words have some impact on our psychological and physical states, it is prolonged exposure—as Newberg and Waldman point out—that makes the most difference. The key, therefore, is to be very selective about the words we read slowly and repeatedly.

Come up with a mantra, a single word that moves you, and say it to yourself once or repeatedly for a minute or two in the morning when you wake up or a few times throughout the day. You may choose any word that inspires you, that evokes positive thoughts and feelings—such as *God* or *grandmother*, *love* or *kindness*, *joy* or *playfulness*, *presence* or *acceptance*. You can wear a bracelet or a necklace to remind you to think of that word, or even a piece of jewelry with the word engraved on it.

Going beyond a single word, identify a quote that inspires you, a poem that moves you, or a paragraph that elevates you. Read it slowly and deliberately, reflecting on what it means to you and how it relates to your life. Then revisit the words the following day, and each day after for a week or longer. This happy habit can be a shared experience with a loved one. In our kitchen, we have a book of poems on our dining table. Occasionally, be it when the kids come home from school or over dinner, one of us reads a poem out loud.

The internet, with all its downsides, is also a treasure trove of inspiring words. Surfing the web, you can find an abundance of inspiring quotes on just about any topic you choose. Reading books or watching movies, you will inevitably come across meaningful sentences or paragraphs worth cherishing. When you come across such words in a religious text, novel, self-help book, or movie, write them down so you can read and reread them. By doing so, you derive the full benefit from them rather than allowing the overload of information to dilute their potency.

There are various factors that render a sentence or a paragraph worthy of your selection. First, it generates positive feelings, giving birth to pleasurable emotions such as joy or excitement or passion. Second, it generates worthy thoughts, guiding you in the direction of your ideals, pointing the way to a better version of yourself and your life. Words you deliberate on often and much can provide you with a reminder of the way you want to feel, think, and most importantly, act.[76]

Words you deliberate on often and much can provide you with a reminder of the way you want to feel, think, and most importantly, act.

Exercise: Read Quotes

Identify a quote or two, a paragraph or two, and spend a couple of minutes reading and rereading them, reflecting on the meaning and purpose of the words. Repeat this exercise each day, going over the same words for an entire week, or much longer if you find it useful. If the words continue to inspire you, print them out and hang them on the wall or use them as a screen saver. Remember that words create worlds.

Appreciative Questions

Questions begin a quest. The kinds of questions we ask determine the nature of the quest we embark on. Asking questions is something we naturally do, and that's a good thing, because it helps us learn and grow. Less helpful, especially when facing difficulties and hardships, is our tendency to limit our questions to those about what isn't working—to inquire exclusively about the empty part of the glass and disregard the full part. For example, if I'm going through a difficult time, the question I'm likely to ask or be asked is, "What's not going well in your life?" If my partner and I are struggling, we and others might ask, "What's not working in the relationship?" And if a company isn't meeting its goals, the questions that management or external consultants usually ask revolve around the organization's shortcomings.

The kinds of questions we ask determine the nature of the quest we embark on.

These are valid, important questions, but mounting evidence suggests that focusing on the problems is not enough. If we want to fulfill our potential, whether personally, interpersonally, or organizationally, we need to go beyond the flaws, deficits, shortcomings, and weaknesses. We need to inquire into what is working, drawing attention to that which is going well.[77]

In the 1970s, David Cooperrider and his colleagues gave birth to a new field of study and practice: Appreciative Inquiry. As its name suggests, Appreciative Inquiry uses positive questions to focus our attention on the half-full part of the glass. In their book *Appreciative Inquiry*, David Cooperrider and Diana Whitney write: "We find that the more positive the question we ask, the more long-lasting and successful the change effort. The major thing a change

agent can do that makes a difference is to craft and ask
unconditional positive questions."[78]

When going through a difficult time, it may be helpful to ask
yourself *What is going well in my life?* In the
midst of interpersonal struggle, there's room
to ask *What is working in this relationship?*
And when the going gets tough at work, it
is helpful to inquire into the organization's
strengths. Whether personally or professionally, to fulfill your potential for learning
and growing, you need to ask positive questions of yourself and of others.

Whether personally or
professionally, to fulfill
your potential for
learning and growing,
you need to ask posi-
tive questions of your-
self and of others.

Executive leadership coach Marshall Goldsmith suggests
asking yourself the following six questions daily:

1. Did I do my best to set clear goals?
2. Did I do my best to make progress toward goal
   achievement?
3. Did I do my best to be happy?
4. Did I do my best to find meaning?
5. Did I do my best to build positive relationships?
6. Did I do my best to be fully engaged?

The reason these questions begin with *Did I do my best
to . . .* is to prevent the blame game and instead take respon-
sibility.[79] These may not be the right questions for you to ask,
but coming up with daily questions—even one or two—can
be incredibly helpful for personal development.

Another set of helpful questions can focus us on our intellectual development:

1. What am I looking forward to learning today?
2. How can I look at a familiar situation from a different
   perspective today?

3. What interesting things did I learn today?
4. What interesting questions can I ask myself tomorrow?

The sky is the limit as far as generating helpful questions that you can ask yourself, be it as a one-off practice or as a daily routine on an ongoing basis.

It is important to point out that abstaining from asking questions concerning the things that are not working—the problems and deficits—is not the path to flourishing. Rather, it's about complementing these questions with appreciative ones. It's about looking at reality, the positive and the negative, paying attention to the glass in its entirety—the part that is empty and the part that is full.

As the research in appreciative inquiry demonstrates, we create our world with the questions that we ask.[80] Therefore, if we are to create the best possible world for ourselves and others, we need to ask questions that highlight the best.

Exercise: Ask Appreciative Questions

Come up with appreciative questions that focus on what is working for you personally, interpersonally, and professionally. Write these questions down and reflect on them when you wake up or at any time during the day. Add new questions or revise old questions whenever you feel the need to do so.

Journaling

Karen Horney, a psychoanalyst who was both a student and a critic of Freud, published her book *Self-Analysis* in 1942.[81] In the book, Horney presents a strong case for the value of journaling. While self-analysis is no substitute for therapy, it is nevertheless an effective and accessible method that can help alleviate psychological distress as well as support personal growth.

While self-analysis is no substitute for therapy, it is nevertheless an effective and accessible method that can help alleviate psychological distress as well as support personal growth.

In 1997, University of Texas psychologist Jamie Pennebaker published his book *Opening Up*, introducing compelling research on the value of journaling. He found that writing continuously for twenty minutes about "the most upsetting or traumatic experience of your entire life" on four consecutive days significantly reduced long-term anxiety, strengthened the immune system, improved mood, and led to more open and social behavior. In another study, Pennebaker gave similar instructions to individuals who had been laid off. Compared to a control group, those who journaled about their experience of being fired and out of work were better off psychologically and received significantly more job offers in subsequent months.[82]

Psychologists Chad Burton and Laura King extended Pennebaker's findings on the value of journaling to include positive life events. Subjects who wrote about their peak experiences for fifteen minutes each time on three consecutive days were happier and healthier, psychologically and physically better off, than those who did not.[83]

Next, Burton and King wanted to test the lower boundary of the dosage of journaling. How much was enough to impact real change? In their study, participants journaled for two minutes on two consecutive days—a total of four minutes of writing. One group was asked to write about traumatic experiences, a second group was asked to write about positive experiences, and a third group was a control group that wrote about neutral experiences. A month after they wrote, participants in the first two groups were still enjoying better health than those in the control group. Four minutes of journaling![84]

In a perfect world, each of us could have a therapist or a coach or a trusted other whom we could speak to about whatever is on our minds and hearts. However, if you can't have or don't want to have such intimate encounters, or even if you do have them and would like to amplify the impact of your time together, journaling may be the thing for you. Expressing what you feel and what you think in writing for fifteen or twenty minutes can be great, but even two short minutes can go a long way.

Expressing what you feel and what you think in writing for fifteen or twenty minutes can be great, but even two short minutes can go a long way.

Exercise: Journal

On two consecutive days, take two minutes to journal about anything that is bothering you, that is weighing you down. You can also write for two minutes on two consecutive days on a positive life experience. If you're moved to continue beyond the two minutes, by all means do so.

When you journal, there's no need to be concerned about grammar or spelling. Free associate; express whatever is on your mind and in your heart. There is no need to journal daily or even weekly. Put pen to paper, or fingers to keyboard, whenever you feel the need to share, to figure something out, or to simply lift your mood.

Curiosity

There are a number of benefits to being curious. People who ask questions and seek to learn new things are more successful overall. They perform better as students in school and as employees in the workplace. They also tend to be happier, with lower levels of anxiety and higher levels of life satisfaction.[85] Finally, curiosity also contributes to our physical health. In their research, Gary Swan and Dorit Carmelli demonstrated that, after controlling for other factors, aging adults who are curious are likely to live longer than those who are not.[86]

People who ask questions and seek to learn new things are more successful overall.

But what if you are not curious? What if you've lost that loving feeling toward learning new things? You're in luck, because in the same way that for as long as we live, we don't lose our desire to eat, we never lose our desire to learn. When it comes to food, we might not like sardines or cucumbers, but we are so constituted that we derive pleasure from eating at least some things. Similarly, we might not like studying mathematics or ancient languages, but our nature dictates that we are capable of deriving pleasure from learning some things.

in the same way that for as long as we live, we don't lose our desire to eat, we never lose our desire to learn.

Your desire to learn new things may be diminished, reduced to a spark rather than burning fiercely within you. To rekindle the fire, to reignite or reinforce your love for learning, all you need to do is pay attention to the treasures of knowledge and wisdom that are often hidden in plain sight. Ask friends or colleagues questions in the areas of their expertise or take a minute to learn some fun fact about a new topic. Since the spark of curiosity is already there, it won't be long before the passion for learning is reignited.

You can also ignite the spark in areas with which you are intimately familiar. In yoga and meditation, even the most experienced practitioners are urged to assume the state of a "beginner's mind."[87] Psychologist Ellen Langer has conducted years of research exploring how we can actively enter this state of a beginner's mind.[88] She instructs participants in her studies to simply "draw novel distinctions"—to notice things that they haven't noticed before, whether in a person, a piece of music, an object, or a situation. Langer encourages people to look for novelty even in something they have no interest in and would normally pay no attention to, or in something with which they are intimately familiar and about which they assume there is nothing new for them to notice.

As a result of entering a beginner's mind—a state of active mindfulness, as Langer describes it—people enjoy increased levels of happiness and health, greater satisfaction in both new and long-standing relationships, higher self-esteem and motivation, and improved memory and learning as well as creativity. Langer's recommendation is to live each day as if it's your first.[89]

Exercise: Be Curious

Indulge your curiosity. Spend one minute learning something new by asking someone a question or by searching online.

In addition, spend a few seconds or longer drawing novel distinctions about something that you are familiar with. Look for novelty in the face of a person you know well, in the content of your own room, while observing a work of art that hangs on your wall, or as you listen to your favorite song. Find the new in the familiar.

We've explored the four happy habits relating to intellectual wellbeing—Words, Quotes, and Excerpts; Appreciative Questions; Journaling; and Curiosity. There are, of course, many more MVIs that fall under the I of SPIRE, from briefly sharing with others something you've just learned to solving a crossword puzzle, from watching a brief video that can teach you something to spending a few minutes a day expanding your vocabulary, from spending two minutes reflecting on what you've learned during the day to asking friends to share with you something new they've learned recently.

The next chapter revolves around relational wellbeing. We'll explore how we can introduce small changes in our homes and in our organizations and, by doing so, enjoy significant positive change in our personal and professional relationships.

The VIVID App: Intellectual Wellbeing Plan

You can scan this QR code for quick access to the exercises from this chapter.

7

Relational Wellbeing MVIs

> Little deeds of kindness,
> Little words of love,
> Make our earth happy,
> Like the Heaven above.

> —Julia Abigail Fletcher Carney[90]

Relational wellbeing is about our deep-seated need for social interactions. The number-one predictor of happiness is spending quality time with people we care about and who care about us.[91] The four happy habits described in this chapter are:

➤ Relationship Boosters
➤ Hugs
➤ Acts of Kindness
➤ Listening

Relationship Boosters

As their name suggests, relationship boosters are happy habits that are unique to relationships. In a fascinating series of

In the best relationships, partners enjoy a 5:1 positivity ratio.

studies, John Gottman demonstrated that in the best relationships, partners enjoy a 5:1 positivity ratio.[92] This means that for every one disagreement or conflict, angry exchange or disappointment, there are five positives—a compliment or a loving text message, a smile, a hug, or a meaningful conversation. Needless to say, determining the 5:1 ratio is challenging, because it's not clear how one assigns a numerical value to each experience. A peck on the cheek, for instance, is unlikely to contribute as much to the positive side of the ratio as a passionate night of lovemaking. A minor disagreement over a trivial matter doesn't affect the negative side of the ratio as much as a serious argument that spans weeks. Moreover, the ratio is an average across relationships rather than a precise prescription for each and every relationship. You can have a wonderful relationship if you're at 4:1 or 7:1.

In what ways, then, is Gottman's ratio helpful? First of all, the existence of a ratio indicates that conflict is essential and shows that sweeping real issues under the rug is unhealthy for the long-term success of your relationship. Second, for your relationship to flourish, you need more positives than negatives.

Based on his findings, Gottman recommends focusing on accentuating the positive more than eliminating the negative. One way to accentuate the positive is through relationship boosters. These are modest day-to-day activities that raise the positivity ratio in the context of our interactions. An act of kindness or a hug, as discussed previously, can be a relationship booster. Writing a text message to your friend or partner, letting them know that you were thinking of them or how grateful you are for them, can go a long way.

Demonstrating interest is a relationship booster. Ask a family member or a colleague what they're up to and how they're doing, and make sure they understand that you really want to know. You can make a relationship extraordinary by focusing on the ordinary.

An important category of relationship boosters comes in the form of genuine, heartfelt compliments. Actively look for

Actively look for positive things to say about people you care about and who care about you.

positive things to say about people you care about and who care about you. Don't wait for special occasions—a birthday or a holiday—to appreciate them. Mark Twain once wrote, "I can live on a good compliment two weeks with nothing else to eat."[93]

Exercise: Introduce Relationship Boosters

Make a list of relationship boosters that you would like to introduce at home and at work. Sprinkle these boosters across your personal and professional interactions. There are countless gestures that can raise the positivity ratio in the context of your relationships. Pick the ones that you resonate with, that most appeal to you.

Hugs

Too many people in too many places have lost touch with touch. This was the case long before we were struck by COVID and forced into social distancing. And now, despite the pandemic being over, the situation continues to get worse as the virtual takes the place of the real and the metaverse replaces the universe.

One antidote to the widespread touch deprivation is hugging. Virginia Satir, one of the twentieth century's most celebrated psychotherapists, wrote:

We need 4 hugs a day for survival.
We need 8 hugs a day for maintenance.
We need 12 hugs a day for growth.[94]

Satir's words are not mere poetic musings; there is, in fact, mounting scientific evidence pointing to the importance of hugs. Psychologist Jane Clipman asked college students participating in her study to add five extra hugs to their day.[95] The instructions were to engage in a nonsexual, frontal, face-to-face hug with two hands. Women found it easier to incorporate the additional hugs, but men eventually found ways to comply—using a great football maneuver as an excuse for hugging teammates, by embracing family members more often, and so on. After a month, the huggers—men and women—were significantly happier than those in the control group who were not prescribed additional hugs.

Research by Anne Dueren and her colleagues from the University of London demonstrated that the duration of the embrace matters, with a five- or ten-second hug yielding more benefits than a one-second hug.[96] When we hug and are hugged, we release oxytocin, enjoy a better mood, and lower our stress levels. In his podcast *On Purpose*, Jay Shetty recommends spreading hugs that are five to ten seconds long throughout the day as one of the key habits of happy and successful couples.

More generally, touch is an important component of a full and fulfilling life. It is a physical as well as a psychological need, just as food and water and air are. Touch helps babies grow and adults flourish, reduces pain and provides pleasure, strengthens the immune system and alleviates anxiety, cultivates physical wellbeing and fosters resilience. University of Miami professor Tiffany Field has conducted years of research showing that "touch is critical for children's growth, development and health, as well as for adults' physical and mental wellbeing."[97]

Touch is an important component of a full and fulfilling life.

It is hardly a coincidence that cultures that are more tactile—that sanction hugs—are generally happier than cultures where physical contact is scarce. Finland and Colombia, where people freely and readily show affection through touch, consistently rank among the happiest countries in the world. In contrast, North Americans and Brits are among the least tactile people in the world, which partially explains why levels of wellbeing are significantly lower in these countries.[98] According to Tiffany Field, many of the most common psychological problems can be attributed to "touch hunger."[99]

Fortunately, no matter where we are in the world, we can usually increase our touch quotient. Even in places where hugging with acquaintances, let alone strangers, is not the norm, it is usually possible to increase the quantity and quality of hugs within our close circle of friends and family.

There are, of course, different kinds of hugs that are appropriate in different contexts and with different people. How close or distant are we? How soft or firm is the hug? How short or how long do we remain embraced? The key is that both people benefit from the hug and that both feel fully comfortable. When touch is consensual and when our own and others' boundaries are respected, we enjoy a win-win connection. When we touch, we too are touched.

When we touch, we too are touched.

Exercise: Hug More!

Find ways to gradually and sensitively incorporate more hugs and more touch throughout your days. When possible and appropriate, extend some of the hugs to ten seconds or even longer. Relax into the hug, focus on the sensations, appreciate yourself and the other.

Acts of Kindness

To give is to receive. One of the most powerful ways to boost our own happiness is by contributing to others' happiness. Why is that? First, our nature dictates that we feel better about ourselves when we give, when we help in one way or another. Second, when we give to others, our relationship with them usually improves, and as our relationships get better, we become happier.

One of the most powerful ways to boost our own happiness is by contributing to others' happiness.

A study conducted by Harvard Business School and the University of British Columbia showed that those who were given money and spent it on others—bought a gift for someone else or donated it—enjoyed a larger increase in their level of happiness than those who spent the same amount of money on themselves.[100] Moreover, it's not just giving money that buys us happiness. Giving something intangible, like kindness, has a similar effect.

In her research, psychologist Sonja Lyubomirsky asked participants to commit a handful of extra acts of kindness each week—being slightly more generous than they normally would be. They could help a colleague at work, spend time with a friend in need, volunteer in a shelter, or just be extra nice to a stranger. This seemingly trivial intervention led to a significant increase in participants' wellbeing.[101] And the nice thing about acts of kindness is that they are always within our reach. Back in the 1940s, Anne Frank wrote in her diary, "You can always, always give something, even if it is only kindness."[102] Being kind to someone is an act of giving that has value for the receiver, the giver, and the world.

No less important than being kind to others is being kind to yourself. If your

No less important than being kind to others is being kind to yourself.

kindness excludes yourself—if your only focus is on helping others—then you'll end up shortchanging yourself as well as others. For kindness to be sustainable, you have to take your own needs into consideration. As the Dalai Lama pointed out, "Caring for others based only on your sacrifice doesn't last. Caring must also feed you."[103]

It is easy to be kind; generosity is part of our nature. Sometimes all we need is a reminder—a bracelet we associate with kindness, a picture of a benevolent person on our wall, a recurring message on our smartphone—to bring out the goodness that awaits inside.

Exercise: Be Kind

Commit to five or more extra acts of kindness each week. You can pick a day to do them all or spread them evenly across the week. Acts of kindness can be premeditated or spontaneous. You can decide in advance how you will help someone, or you can do so when opportunity presents itself. And remember to treat yourself as you treat others—with kindness.

Listening

Listening is one of the most potent forms of giving, of being kind and generous. Research by Hiroaki Kawamichi, Osnat Boskila-Yam, and others shows the benefits of listening—to the listener and to the one being listened to.[104]

Listening to another person with mindful intention can contribute to relational wellbeing by leading to a deeper connection between two people. Children who are listened to—by their parents, teachers, or friends—grow up to be more confident adults.[105] In the workplace, employees who feel heard and understood, whose managers are mindful listeners, experience less stress, are healthier, and miss fewer days of work. When working in teams, employees who listen well to each other perform better and are more satisfied at work.[106]

Listening to another person with mindful intention can contribute to relational wellbeing by leading to a deeper connection between two people.

What can you do to become a better listener? In her book *The Zen of Listening*, Rebecca Shafir employs the metaphor of watching a movie to explain the art and science of effective listening.[107] Think about it! What is unique about the experience of going to the movies, and how is it different relative to other situations? First, you do not interrupt. You allow the story to unfold, the characters to do and say their thing. To interrupt would be both futile and rude to the other moviegoers. Second, you seek to understand. You are genuinely interested in what the characters are saying, doing, thinking, and feeling. By the end of the movie, you have a pretty good picture, so to speak, of what the characters are about. Third, given that you do not interrupt and genuinely seek to understand, you pay attention. You are present, absorbed in the here and now. Finally, you let go. Given that you can't really change the trajectory of the movie, you let go of trying to change the characters. You are simply there to empathize—feeling their pain and enduring their struggles, experiencing their joy, and celebrating their feats.

Not interrupting, seeking to understand, paying attention, and letting go are great guidelines for effective listening. You know how to watch a movie—you know what it feels like and what it requires of you. Now apply this

Not interrupting, seeking to understand, paying attention, and letting go are great guidelines for effective listening.

knowledge to the way you listen to your friend, family member, colleague, or anyone else. And then listen to yourself!

Just as is the case for kindness in general, so it is for listening, for when you give, you receive, and when you serve, you gain. As Shafir writes, "truly listening, forgetting yourself for a short time, and getting into the speaker's movie can be the kindest gift you can give to another." Shafir then points out that by listening, we do not merely offer a gift to others; we do so for ourselves as well: "If we approach a listening opportunity with the same self-abandonment as we do at the movies, think of how much more we stand to gain from these encounters."[108]

Fred Rogers, the beloved host of *Mister Rogers' Neighborhood*, practiced a powerful relational MVI directly related to listening: Before responding in a conversation, he would take a moment to pause.[109] This simple, silent act, usually lasting no more than a few seconds to a minute, allowed him to carefully consider what he just heard and then ensure his response was compassionate and thoughtful.

Exercise: Listen Mindfully

Create reminders to be a better, more mindful, listener. Commit to being present for one minute as you spend time with a friend or a colleague. This one minute will often extend to the next minute and to the one after as you become more present to others and to yourself.

The four happy habits in this chapter—relationship boosters, hugs, acts of kindness, and listening—are brief yet powerful practices that can significantly enhance happiness levels. Additional MVIs that can deepen and enrich your relationships include sharing a genuine compliment or a genuine smile with another person, doing a one-minute lovingkindness meditation by yourself or with a friend, going out of your way to celebrate a friend's or a family member's success, reconnecting with a person you've lost touch with or connecting to a person you're close to by opening up and showing vulnerability, taking a deep breath before responding in conflict, or identifying and acknowledging a strength in another person.

In the next chapter we shift to the final SPIRE element, emotional wellbeing, as we look at how we can deal with painful emotions as well as generate more pleasurable ones.

The VIVID App: Relational Wellbeing Plan

You can scan this QR code to directly access the exercises from this chapter.

8

Emotional Wellbeing MVIs

The best and most beautiful things in the world
cannot be seen or even touched. They must be
felt with the heart.

—Helen Keller[110]

Emotional wellbeing is about learning to deal with painful emotions—such as anger, anxiety, sadness, and envy—and cultivating pleasurable emotions such as joy, love, gratitude, and excitement. The four happy habits described in this chapter are:

➤ Accepting Emotions
➤ Changing Perspective
➤ Expressing Gratitude
➤ Pleasure Boosters

Accepting Emotions

The first step toward happiness is allowing in unhappiness. To lead a full and fulfilling life, you need to first give yourself permission to be human.[111]

To lead a full and fulfilling life, you need to first give yourself permission to be human.

The belief that you—or anyone else, for that matter—can lead a life devoid of painful emotions is misguided and harmful and constitutes perhaps the most significant barrier to happiness. The paradox is that when you reject painful emotions, they escalate and intensify. In contrast, when you accept them, they dissipate and depart. Moreover, when you invite in the painful, you open yourself up to the pleasurable—for all emotions flow through a single pipeline, and by blocking the path of sadness, you inadvertently obstruct joy. It is only when you give yourself the permission to be human—when you accept that feeling fear, anger, sadness, or envy is an inevitable part of being alive—that you can fulfill your potential for both psychological and physical health. Life as a whole becomes so much lighter and more peaceful when rather than fighting your nature, you embrace it—pain, pleasure, and all.

But how do you give yourself permission to be human? How do you embrace your emotions? Given that emotions manifest themselves in our mind and in our body, we need to accept our thoughts and our physical sensations. Take anxiety preceding a presentation at work, for example. You may be asking yourself *What if I fail?* or *What will they think of me?* You may be thinking *This is really scary!* or *I am going to bomb the presentation!* In terms of physical sensations, you may experience anxiety as a knot in your belly, tension in your forehead, or tightness in your throat.

The key to acceptance is to bear witness to the emotion without judgment or censure, without trying to get rid of it or change it in any way. In the words of Oxford professor Mark Williams, it is about observing the thoughts and the physical sensations with "friendly curiosity."[112] As you observe the emotion, it may flow freely through you and out of you, leaving just as it came. Alternatively, it may linger for a little longer, in which case, welcome it with an open heart.

> *The key to acceptance is to bear witness to the emotion without judgment or censure, without trying to get rid of it or change it in any way.*

You can practice this form of acceptance during set times—say, for a minute or two in the morning, or in bed before you fall asleep. Alternatively, you can practice acceptance whenever the need arises. For example, if you feel anxiety before a presentation or envy when you're about to spend time with a friend, take a minute to simply and nonjudgmentally observe the thoughts going through your mind and the physical sensations in your body.

Exercise: Observe Your Emotions

Once a day, spend a minute or two observing whatever emotion is present in your mind and your body. If no distinct emotion rises to the surface, scan your body for any part that may be a little tense or uncomfortable and simply observe that part with friendly curiosity. Give yourself permission to be human by unconditionally accepting any and all emotions.

Changing Perspective

What do you see in this picture?

This image, taken from an 1892 German humor magazine, can either be seen as a duck or as a rabbit.[113] Do you see it? Once you recognize both animals for the first time, you'll always be able to see them. This image has been used by psychologists to illustrate a simple truth with important implications: Distinct perspectives of the same phenomenon may be equally valid and yet produce radically different outcomes.

> *Distinct perspectives of the same phenomenon may be equally valid and yet produce radically different outcomes.*

In a groundbreaking study on cognitive framing, New Mexico State University psychologist Joe Tomaka identified students who normally experienced high levels of stress before an exam.[114] The students were randomly divided into two groups prior to taking a test. The first group was told that the task was "difficult mental arithmetic" and were instructed to complete it efficiently and quickly. As a result, these students appraised the test as *threatening*. Participants in the second group were given a "mental arithmetic" task and told that they should try hard to do their best. Rather than viewing the test as threatening, they saw it as *challenging*.

Just as the same picture can be seen as either a duck or as a rabbit, the same test can be perceived as either threatening or challenging. The way students appraised the task—whether as a threat or as a challenge—made a difference: Students in the second group were significantly calmer and more creative and actually performed better on the test.

This is just one of many studies that confirm that a single word can have a dramatic impact on how well we perform, how healthy we are, and how we experience our life.[115] A public lecture can primarily be about seeking validation from the

> *A single word can have a dramatic impact on how well we perform, how healthy we are, and how we experience our life.*

audience or about sharing what you care about with others.[116] A bedtime routine with a child can be perceived as an obligation or as a privilege. Work can be experienced as a job or as a calling.[117]

Sometimes—not always, but sometimes—even inherently difficult situations can be reframed. We can see failure as a disaster or as a learning opportunity.[118] A conflict within a relationship can be a menace or a door to cultivating intimacy by learning about each other.[119]

The first step is to write down a statement that captures the reframed perspective. The second step is to reinforce this new perspective by rereading the statement. For example, you can write, "Speaking in front of an audience is an opportunity to share what I care about with others," and then reread it each morning or just before an upcoming lecture.

The brilliant British novelist Mary Ann Evans wrote, "It is a narrow mind which cannot look at a subject from various points of view."[120] At least to some extent, how you evaluate—and hence how you experience—situations is up to you. What you focus on doesn't merely reflect reality, it also creates reality.

Exercise: Reframe a Situation

Think of a situation in your life that you experience as threatening or negative in any way. In writing, reframe the situation as challenging, as an opportunity, or in any other positive way. Reread your reframed statement at specific times during the day or whenever you feel the need to do so. Focus on the emotions that the new perspective elicits. You may consider visualizing yourself in the situation, enjoying yourself, having a positive experience.

Expressing Gratitude

The Roman statesman and philosopher Marcus Tullius Cicero referred to gratitude as "not only the greatest of virtues, but also the mothers of all others."[121] We live in a wonder-full world, and there is so much that we can be grateful for. Yet most of us take much of what we have for granted.

> *We live in a wonder-full world, and there is so much that we can be grateful for.*

In a study conducted by psychologists Robert Emmons and Michael McCullough, participants were asked to write down five things, big or small, for which they were grateful. It turns out that beyond being more grateful about life as a whole, participants who persisted over a period of a few weeks were more joyful, energetic, and helpful to others. They also slept better and experienced fewer symptoms of physical illness.[122]

How is it that such a simple and brief intervention can lead to such significant benefits? Emmons and McCullough suggest that being grateful triggers an upward spiral of growth and well-being. When you take stock of the good things in your life, you feel better. When you feel better, you become more open to—and are more likely to pursue—positive experiences. You then have more to be grateful for, which in turn improves the quality of your life, and so on.

The word *appreciate* has two meanings—to be grateful for something and to grow in value. These two meanings are intimately connected, for when you appreciate the good, the good appreciates.

> *When you appreciate the good, the good appreciates.*

Make this practice a ritual. Record your gratitude entry either every night before going to bed or every morning as you open your eyes. Additionally, doing this exercise at the end of a workday and focusing on what went well at work yields significant results in terms of performance and satisfaction. You can decide to do it daily, or if you don't have time or patience to do it every day, even once a week is beneficial.[123]

Expressing gratitude can also be a group activity. Whether around the boardroom table with colleagues or around the dinner table with family and friends, taking turns to express gratitude can contribute to everyone's mental and physical wellbeing.

When expressing gratitude, it is key to be both mindful and heartful. To reap the benefits of this simple practice, it's not enough to mechanically "go through the motions" and mindlessly write whatever comes to mind. You have to focus on what you write, experience what it means to you.[124] If a good friend makes your list, bring up her image in your mind's eye and feel her presence. Perhaps you can even think of something specific that you did together that day.

When you make a habit of gratitude, you no longer require a special event to make you happy, because if you really pay attention, you'll realize that there is so much in your life— and in the world—that is worthy of beholding and appreciating.

Exercise: Express Gratitude

Find a regular time during the day to write down three to five things for which you are grateful. You might consider keeping a pen and small notebook by your bed for this purpose. Date each entry so that you can always look back, review, and appreciate your own gratitude history.

Pleasure Boosters

The work of psychologist Barbara Fredrickson illustrates just how important it is for us to experience pleasurable emotions. Fredrickson suggests that emotions like gratitude, love, joy, pride, and awe are not desirable merely because they feel good as ends in themselves but also because they are means toward other ends.[125] When we experience pleasurable emotions, we become more creative and innovative, develop more resilience and a better connection with others, and enjoy better health as well as extra energy and vitality.

> *When we experience pleasurable emotions, we become more creative and innovative, develop more resilience and a better connection with others, and enjoy better health as well as extra energy and vitality.*

Many of the MVIs discussed throughout this book elevate our emotions and contribute to our overall experience of pleasure—whether it be in a meditation session or following a cold shower, after opening up in our journal or during a hug. In this respect, this final happy habit is a way of bringing all the others together.

Specifically, a pleasure booster is a bite-sized activity that elevates your mood. This can be about closing your eyes for a minute and imagining a person you love or listening to a favorite song, savoring a bite over lunch or taking a minute to read a poem that moves you, rolling on the floor with your dog or watching a short video clip of cute cats. Introduce these special moments throughout your life. In the words of Nathaniel Branden, "pleasure for man is not a luxury, but a profound psychological need."[126]

To enjoy these pleasure boosters, we need to stop and take our time, even if it is for a minute or thirty seconds. Abayomi

Omoogun from the University of Texas points out that "when you stop rushing and slow down, you enjoy life more. Things are more interesting. You worry less. You care for others more."[127] So why don't we slow down more often? The reason so many of us are reluctant to stop and savor has to do with a mindset that glorifies delaying gratification and equates slowness with laziness. While delaying gratification is at times important, it is equally important to seize the moment and indulge ourselves with a pleasure booster—even when, or especially when, it seems like we don't have a moment to spare. If we delay gratification indefinitely, we end up with no gratification at all, because we don't live indefinitely.

If we delay gratification indefinitely, we end up with no gratification at all, because we don't live indefinitely.

As I mentioned at the beginning of the book, I enjoyed the most significant increase in my happiness levels not because of the large and major changes that I made in my life but rather as a result of the seemingly minor interventions I introduced. Just as, in the words of German art historian Aby Warburg, "God is in the details," so it is that happiness is in the details.[128] Pleasure boosters are those small gifts that we give ourselves that keep on giving, as they generate upward spirals in our life.

Exercise: List Your Pleasure Boosters

Make a list of pleasure boosters, bite-sized activities that elevate your mood. Introduce these throughout your day, week, and month so that you can make the most of your life and enjoy the many benefits that come with enjoyment.

Accepting emotions, changing perspective, expressing gratitude, and pleasure boosters are the four MVIs I elaborated on in this chapter. These barely scratch the surface of happy habits that can significantly enhance emotional wellbeing. You can activate your parasympathetic system by placing your hand on your heart for thirty seconds or release feel-good hormones by taking a minute to watch something that makes you laugh. You can look at a picture of a puppy, a kitten, a baby, or anything or anyone that makes you smile in appreciation; you can hum a calming tune or listen to a song that elicits strong emotions in you.

We are now ready to move to the third and final part of this book. You will learn how the 3 Rs of Change—reminders, repetition, and rituals—can help you make the MVIs an integral part of your life so that you can enjoy positive and lasting change.

The VIVID App: Emotional Wellbeing Plan

You can scan this QR code for direct access to the exercises from this chapter.

PART 3

Lasting Change Through the 3 Rs

9

The 3 Rs of Change

All big things come from small beginnings. The
seed of every habit is a single, tiny decision. But
as that decision is repeated, a habit sprouts and
grows stronger.

—James Clear[129]

MVIs are unique in the rich landscape of psychological interventions. First, unlike many of the interventions within the
self-help universe, they are evidence based, derived from
research. This does not in any way imply that you should
blindly follow the dictates in this book and straightaway introduce all the happy habits into your life. Not everything that
comes out of research labs stands the test of time; scientists are
human and therefore fallible.

Moreover, research in psychology usually derives conclu-
sions that apply to the average person or to the majority. A
particular intervention, therefore, may work splendidly for
most people but not at all for you. However, the fact that the
MVIs are evidence based makes a good case for your trying
them out, experimenting with them, and ascertaining for
yourself whether they do or don't work. As I mentioned earlier,
complement research with mesearch.

The second unique aspect of the MVIs, which I previously
discussed, is that they're relatively easy and straightforward to

implement and pose a low barrier to entry. Putting aside a minute or two—for journaling, meditating, rereading a quote, or jumping up and down—is a lot easier and more likely to happen than dedicating twenty minutes or an hour to similar activities. They also provide an antidote to the *all-or-nothing* approach to change.

Too many people lead a sedentary lifestyle because they believe that if they can't commit to a full-on exercise regime, they may as well do nothing. Too many partners forgo precious moments together because they only see value in spending a full day together or at the very least a prolonged dinner date. And way too many people forgo a mindfulness practice because they believe that anything short of a thirty-minute meditation session is useless. While a full-on exercise regime, a prolonged date, and a half hour of daily meditation are great and important, there is much that can be done in the space between all and nothing.

And yet, the fact that the happy habits I've introduced you to are evidence based and the fact that they pose a relatively low barrier to entry doesn't mean that making them an integral part of your life is an easy endeavor that just happens because you read this book. Time, effort, commitment, and dedication are all necessary if you are to derive the potential benefits inherent in the MVIs.

Time, effort, commitment, and dedication are all necessary if you are to derive the potential benefits inherent in the MVIs.

Knowing Is Not Enough

Most change efforts—whether personal or organizational—fail, because most people misunderstand what it takes to bring about lasting change. When it comes to the question of how to bring about lasting change in your life, it turns out that, by and large, philosophers had it wrong and theologians had it right. The philosophers' error is epitomized by Socrates, considered the father of Western philosophy, who believed that to know the good is to do the good. In other words, Socrates believed that once you know what the right thing to do is, you will do it.[130] This assumption is sadly false.

Knowing does not in and of itself guarantee doing, and while it is surely an important and necessary first step, it is far from sufficient. Many people know the tangible benefits of an active lifestyle yet fail to engage in physical exercise. The majority of people living in developed countries know which food is

> *Knowing does not in and of itself guarantee doing, and while it is surely an important and necessary first step, it is far from sufficient.*

good for them but nevertheless continue to consume unhealthy food in large quantities. The fact that so many of us take for granted much of what life has to offer is not because we don't know that in every way gratitude is better for us than ingratitude. Generally, we know how we ought to treat our child, partner, or colleague, yet our behavior often falls short of our knowledge. We know what to do but often fail to do it.[131]

While not all philosophers subscribe to Socrates's notion that knowledge is sufficient to inspire action—Aristotle and Confucius, for instance, rejected this idea—it was largely religion that presented the alternative approach. Theologians throughout the ages recognized the philosophers' error and effectively bridged the theory-practice gap. If the coveted destination is virtuous action, then

> *The 3 Rs—reminders, repetition, and rituals—are essential for attaining real and lasting change.*

knowledge is merely a first step in the journey.[132] Thousands of years of religious practice, coupled with more recent research in psychology and neuroscience, has demonstrated that the 3 Rs—reminders, repetition, and rituals—are essential for attaining real and lasting change.

Reminders

In the context of bringing about change, *reminders* are external cues in our environment that focus our attention on a particular commitment we made. Some reminders are straightforward and simple; others are a little more complicated and creative. For example, a bracelet that you always or periodically wear on your wrist can be a reminder to return to the present moment and engage in informal meditation (a Spiritual Wellbeing MVI) regardless of what you're doing. If you would like to engage in regular high-intensity exercise bursts (a Physical Wellbeing MVI), you can set your smartphone to ping every two hours. A question mark or the word *QUESTION* or a quote about the importance of inquiry on your screen saver can be a reminder to regularly ask appreciative questions (an Intellectual Wellbeing MVI). A picture of your mother or of Mother Teresa can remind you to consistently engage in acts of kindness (a Relational Wellbeing MVI). You can use your daily planner to remind you to express gratitude (an Emotional Wellbeing MVI) at the end of each day.

Within religion, reminders manifest themselves in a few ways. For instance, the primary function of prayer, which is an integral part of most religions, is not to engender knowing—certainly not after the prayer has been read several times and has been committed to memory. Instead, prayer serves as a reminder of the values and changes that a religion aspires to develop in the individual and the community.

Another example of reminding, within religion, comes in the form of special holidays. Catholics are encouraged to observe Saint Augustine Day on August 28 as a way of reminding themselves of Augustinian values. Passover, for Jews, is a reminder of the journey they took thousands of years ago from slavery to freedom. Moreover, merely attending temple, church, or mosque services provides a reminder—through words, music, and visual aids—of the creeds and conduct that each religion seeks to inspire and inculcate.

We can categorize reminders into two types, those relating to our attitudes and those that target our behaviors. Attitude reminders focus by and large on our *internal* world of thoughts and feelings. For example, I may choose to remind myself that I am kind, that I accept my emotions unconditionally, that I appreciate the good in myself and others, or that I am a loving parent. Behavior reminders focus on the *external* world of deeds and acts. For example, I may need a reminder to donate to charity, exercise regularly, breathe deeply, or listen patiently when my children talk.

> *We can categorize reminders into two types, those relating to our attitudes and those that target our behaviors.*

Attitude and behavior reminders are interconnected, sometimes representing two sides of the same change coin. They can, and often do, work together and reinforce each other. For example, reminding myself to be a loving parent works alongside reminding myself to patiently listen to my children. Being self-confident can reinforce and be reinforced by my saying no to things that are not aligned with my values. Additionally, setting a reminder to donate to charity every Friday and regularly reminding myself that I am a caring person target the same desired outcome of increasing kindness.

Repetition

Regular reminders can pave the way to *repetition*, which is of course essential for lasting change.[133] Engaging in a meditation practice for seven straight days is unlikely to significantly impact your overall physical and psychological wellbeing. To become physically stronger or more flexible takes time and doesn't happen overnight or even over a month. Journaling once or twice can certainly help, but the significant benefits of self-analysis come when we journal consistently. Introducing relationship boosters for a week or two is unlikely to bring about deep change within your relationship and life. And giving yourself permission to be human has to be an ongoing practice if you are to meaningfully move the happiness needle.

Sporadic reminders aren't enough to bring about lasting change. Both attitude and behavior reminders need to be evoked regularly and consistently to have a real impact. This is why most religions encourage members to repeat particular prayers daily, attend services at least once a week, and celebrate the same holidays consistently year in and year out. Without repetition of both actions and words, new behaviors and attitudes are unlikely to stick.[134]

Without repetition of both actions and words, new behaviors and attitudes are unlikely to stick.

If you repeatedly commit acts of kindness, you become kinder over time. If you consistently engage in physical exercise, you not only become fitter, you also internalize the value of exercising and therefore are likely to exercise more. And if you make a point of expressing love—whether by listening more intently or hugging more frequently—you become more loving. In the words of Will Durant, "we are what we repeatedly do."[135]

When you repeat certain words, over time you internalize them and they become part of you. Eknath Easwaran, the English professor who in 1968 taught the first academic course on meditation in the United States, suggested that part of your daily meditation ought to include a passage you find meaningful and inspiring. With each repetition, says

Easwaran, we drive these words "deeper and deeper into our subconscious . . . the truths the passages express simply become part of one's life, assimilated into character and consciousness just as the nutrients in food become part of the body. In the simplest possible language, this is the secret of meditation: we become what we meditate on."[136] We become what we repeatedly say.

Individuals as well as entire cultures are shaped by words that are repeated to them and by them. On the individual level, what our parents and teachers tell us—and what we then internalize and tell ourselves—often determines who we become. There is much research under the banner of the Pygmalion Effect illustrating that the message a parent or teacher communicates to a child becomes a self-fulfilling prophecy.[137] Tell a child that she is a capable student and a worthy person, and so it will be. The opposite is unfortunately also true—communicate to a child that he is incompetent and unworthy, and so it will happen.[138]

> *Individuals as well as entire cultures are shaped by words that are repeated to them and by them.*

On a group level, the mindsets and behaviors of entire cultures are determined by words and actions that are repeated. Why, for example, have Jews contributed disproportionally to scholarship and learning throughout history? Why are there so many more Jewish Nobel Prize winners per capita than those of any other cultural or ethnic group? Because Jews have been assigned the title "The People of the Book" and words such as the Biblical verse "And you shall study it day and night" are repeatedly invoked to remind and encourage Jews to study. These phrases, repeated often and much, have become the DNA of the Jewish culture, and through that have determined the destiny of countless individuals within the group who have dedicated their lives to scholarship.

What accounts for the courage and bravery that characterized the Maasai people of Africa for centuries? The words they used to describe themselves—the stories of warriors such as Senteu and Lenana that are repeated—communicate a message that is then internalized. And there are of course acts of bravery or courage that become the fodder for more stories that further reinforce the belief that they are brave and courageous. Positive words lead to positive action; positive action leads to positive words; and so on in a positive upward spiral.

Rituals

When you introduce reminders and repetition into your life, you are getting closer to the promised land of change—the cultivation of rituals.[139] A ritual develops when a neural pathway that is associated with a particular behavior or a thought pattern is formed in the brain. The neural pathway leads you, guides you, to act or think in a certain way at a certain time. For example, after repeatedly reminding yourself to return to the here and now, focusing on the present moment becomes second nature. After taking cold showers for a month or two, the body gets used to this form of shock treatment and begins to crave these experiences. Reading and rereading texts slowly and deliberately over time cultivates the ability and the desire to deeply engage with texts—and with life. Changing perspective becomes almost second nature to you once you have done it regularly over an extended period of time. And while initially you may need a reminder to hug repeatedly, soon it becomes a joyful habit.[140]

When an activity or a way of thinking is repeated often and much, it becomes a habit, a ritual. It no longer requires extraordinary effort as it becomes an effortless part of your ordinary life. As the Irish poet Frederick Langbridge writes in his book *The Happiest Half Hour,* "we are our own potters; for our habits make us, and we make our habits."[141]

A thought, a feeling, or a behavior is ritualized when you do it automatically as a matter of habit without the need for prompts, prods, or persuasion. For a devout individual, appreciating a piece of bread or saying grace before a meal is usually automatic—second nature—as is giving to charity, turning to God for forgiveness, or celebrating a religious holiday. While religion is systematically structured to cultivate rituals, we have all internalized some rituals that are outside the religious domain—brushing our teeth first thing in the morning, putting on our seat belt as we enter a car, watering our plants once a week, or feeling lovingkindness when we see a picture of our grandmother. These rituals emerged from reminders and repetition more than from understanding and knowing. For example, while most of us were told as children how and why it was important to brush our teeth, it was only through our parents reminding us repeatedly to brush our teeth that we internalized the morning ritual.

When an activity or a way of thinking is repeated often and much, it becomes a habit, a ritual.

The Choice to Change

While cells, tissues, and organs form your physical constitution, reminders, repetition, and rituals form your psychological constitution. You inherit your initial physical makeup from evolution and genes and nature; you inherit your initial psychological makeup from parents and teachers and society. Your physical health throughout your life is of course impacted by the initial conditions created by evolution, genes, and nature; however, your choices—how well you eat, rest, and exercise, for example— affect the state of your cells, tissues, and organs and therefore matter a great deal to how long and how well you live.

Similarly, your mental health throughout your life is impacted by the initial conditions that parents, teachers, and society set up for you. This, however, does not negate the fact that your choices throughout your life can and do have a considerable effect on your psychological state. Specifically, what you choose to remind yourself of, what you choose to repeat, and therefore what rituals you choose to create determine how happy and fulfilled you ultimately become.[142]

Theologians understand that it's not sufficient to explain a concept once or twice in a sermon, no matter how charismatically and convincingly it is stated, to bring about lasting change. Therefore, the whole structure of the religious institution revolves around reminders, repetition, and rituals. In contrast, organizations like schools, universities, consulting practices, and training centers that are dedicated to producing individual or organizational change teach under the explicit or implicit assumption that knowledge is the path to change. And they are failing miserably. Psychologist Daniel Goleman, who has dedicated his life to bringing about change in individuals and organizations, points to the failure of most knowledge-driven change efforts: "Although studies have shown that real change can result from training, most of the time the change doesn't seem to be sustained, which is why it is often called the honeymoon effect."[143]

Knowing, on its own, is rarely enough to take you beyond the honeymoon effect. If you want education to bring about sustained impact and to do more than create depositories of facts (you have Google and AI bots for that)—if you are to replace information with transformation—then you must choose to complement knowing and understanding with the 3 Rs of Change.

Knowing, on its own, is rarely enough to take you beyond the honeymoon effect.

The Habitual Animal

When we look at living creatures from an
outward point of view, one of the first things
that strike us is that they are bundles of habits.

—William James[144]

Aristotle, who alongside Socrates is considered the father of Western philosophy, defines a human being as a "rational animal."[145] And just as Socrates's notion that to know the good is to do the good was challenged, so has Aristotle's idea of rationality as our defining characteristic come under attack.

Beyond Our Rational Nature

Philosophers and psychologists throughout history have questioned Aristotle's claim that we are predominantly rational. In research that won him the Nobel Prize in economics, psychologist Daniel Kahneman challenged the "rationality assumption" by pointing to the many irrational decisions that humans make and to the biases and errors that pervade the thinking process.[146] In his *Treatise on Human Nature*, eighteenth-century Scottish philosopher David Hume attempted to dethrone rationality, ironically through a series of rational arguments. Hume concluded that "reason is, and ought only to be the slave of the passions and can never pretend to any other office than to serve and obey them."[147]

Are we, as humans, rational animals? Or are we, perhaps, emotional animals? Aristotle was partially right. We are certainly capable of rational decisions, and some of the choices we make are informed by reason. At the same time, Kahneman's research coupled with Hume's arguments certainly makes a strong case for adding "emotional" to the mix—if not as the only or top adjective describing our nature, then as one of the descriptors, at the very least. After all, many of the things that we choose to do, or not do, are a result of how we feel about them.

There is, though, a missing element in describing our nature, specifically relevant in the context of bringing about change. In addition to being rational and emotional animals, we are also creatures of habit, or habitual animals.[148] And it turns out that to bridge the knowing-doing gap and thus realize our potential for growth and development, we must pay close attention to this third element of our nature.

In addition to being rational and emotional animals, we are also creatures of habit, or habitual animals.

Sixteenth-century British philosopher Francis Bacon pointed out that "nature to be commanded must be obeyed."[149] According to Bacon, to make the most of what life has to offer, you must take your nature into consideration and adhere to it. When you leave out part of your nature—when you dismiss or ignore it rather than recognize and obey it—you are less likely to fulfill your human potential. It is only when you acknowledge your full nature, including your being a creature of habit, that you can fully flourish.

Rhetorical Choices

To explain the need to adhere to our nature as creatures of habit, we can explore the idea of *rhetorical choices*, which are derived from rhetorical questions. A rhetorical question is usually asked for its dramatic effect. The answer to the question tends to be straightforward and obvious. Asking a child whether he wants us to get angry is a rhetorical question—of course he doesn't. Asking a person whether she wants to be happy is also a rhetorical question—of course she does. A rhetorical choice is derived directly from a rhetorical question and therefore presents a situation where the choice between the options is obvious.

> *A rhetorical choice is derived directly from a rhetorical question and therefore presents a situation where the choice between the options is obvious.*

Reflect on the following rhetorical question and ensuing choice. Do you want to appreciate your loved ones, or would you like to take them for granted? I doubt that anyone would say they've had enough of appreciating their beloved family and friends and are now ready to ignore them and take them for granted. And yet most people, most of the time, take their loved ones for granted.

Here is another rhetorical choice. Do you prefer to treat your loved ones with kindness and patience, or would you rather be unkind and impatient? Few if any people would choose the latter option, and yet all of us can think of times when we reacted harshly and insensitively and subsequently regretted our behavior. Why do we so often make such poor choices when the better or more fulfilling choice is clear and known to us? It's because neither the rational part of our nature nor the emotional part is sufficient to determine our actions.

Embracing Our Habitual Nature

To make better choices, if not all of the time then at least more of the time, we have to recognize and obey our nature as creatures of habit—in terms of our attitudes and in terms of our behaviors. To further expand upon the example I mentioned previously, habit is the reason that we pay little attention to, or entirely overlook, good things in our life—including our loved ones. We've been ignoring the good things for so long that a dismissive attitude toward the good things has become second nature to us. Along similar lines, we have responded impatiently or harshly so often before that it is now a matter of habit to persist with this behavior.

There are numerous examples of unhealthy or undesirable habits that we mindlessly engage in, despite knowing better. Why don't we exercise regularly when we know that doing so will make us healthier and happier? It's because we have established a habit of switching on the screen and entering a vegetative state when we get home after work. Why do we chastise ourselves for feeling down or experiencing emotional pain when we know that giving ourselves permission to be human and being more forgiving toward ourselves is the right way to go? Because over the years we have made it a habit to reject our emotions rather than embrace them. And yet no matter how long we have been victims of harmful habits, it is within our power to change them.

The 3 Rs can help us retire detrimental patterns of behavior and replace them with beneficial ones. In his book *Thinking, Fast and Slow*, Daniel Kahneman recognizes the importance of reminders: "Intelligence is not only the ability to reason; it is also the

The 3 Rs can help us retire detrimental patterns of behavior and replace them with beneficial ones.

ability to find relevant material in memory and to deploy attention when needed."[150] If this is indeed true, and there is an abundance of research to suggest that it is, then using reminders helps you become a more intelligent, rational creature with more control over the choices you make.

Sometimes all it takes is a reminder that you have a choice to begin with—whether about being grateful and appreciative or about being kind and patient—to get you to make the rational and emotionally sound decision. Usually, however, to achieve long-term change, reminders alone are not enough. You need to add repetition to the mix so that new habits and new rituals are created. It is through the 3 Rs that you can grow, learn, improve, and become the best version of yourself.

The Double Standard of Change

One of the major barriers to personal development comes from a pervasive double standard that distinguishes how people approach change in psychology versus any other domain. When it comes to psychological growth, most people consciously or subconsciously believe that merely listening to an inspiring podcast or reading a self-help book will change their life for the better. In contrast, few if any would maintain that just reading a book on playing the piano makes one a better pianist. Similarly, most people understand that listening to a podcast with Lebron James is in and of itself insufficient if one seeks to improve as a basketball player. Theoretical knowledge is, at best, a first step along a thousand-mile journey. Investing time and effort actually playing the instrument or on the court is essential if you are to get better, reach farther, and climb higher.

Theoretical knowledge is, at best, a first step along a thousand-mile journey.

Applying a different standard to the realm of self-help—expecting that merely reading books or listening to lectures can lead to personal growth—thwarts the possibility of real and lasting change. Scientist-turned-meditator Matthieu Ricard wrote about this phenomenon:

> We don't find anything strange about spending years learning to walk, to read and write or to acquire professional skills. We spend hours doing physical exercises in order to get our bodies fit. Sometimes we expend tremendous physical energy pedaling a stationary bike that goes nowhere . . . Working with the mind follows the same logic. How could it be subject to change without the least effort, just from wishing alone? That doesn't make any more sense than expecting to learn to play a Mozart sonata just by occasionally doodling around on the piano.[151]

When and Where?

The different MVIs vary greatly in terms of how, and how much, they are employed, depending on their nature as well as on your particular needs and wants. For example, you may choose to implement high-intensity bursts of exercise four times during the day but a gratitude journal once before you go to bed. A happy habit may be triggered by a specific need—you write in your journal when you're feeling stressed—or by circumstance—whenever you have an opportunity to be kind, you seize it. You may join a happy habit to an existing ritual—such as by adding a minute of cold immersion to your daily shower—or have it accessible to you throughout the day—such as by having your favorite quote on the wall. There are countless ways to incorporate the MVIs into your life, and through experimentation over time you will find those that work best for you.

As you remind, repeat, and ritualize, keep two things in mind: First, less is more. You are most likely to succeed if you underreach rather than overreach—modest hopes and aspirations that lead to small wins are the way to go.[152] Second, don't worry if you fail. Each time you make an attempt to introduce a change into your life, regardless of whether or not you succeed, you're reinforcing the neural pathways associated with the particular behavior or thought pattern.[153] Most people don't succeed the first or second time they attempt to introduce a new ritual. Success on the sixth or seventh attempt is much more likely.[154] To truly flourish—to learn and grow and bridge the knowing-doing gap—you need to apply the 3 Rs of Change, and then do it again and again.

11

Just Do It, Again . . .

Success doesn't come from what you do occasionally. It comes from what you do consistently.

—Marie Forleo[155]

Bringing about change is rarely easy. No matter how important
you know the change to be, how motivated you are to see it
through, or how many resolutions you make to uphold it, most
of the time you fail to adopt the new and leave the familiar
behind. An unsuccessful change attempt is not necessarily a
bad thing, since you can learn and grow from failure. Repeatedly falling down can become problematic, however, when it
engenders a sense of helplessness and a belief that you are hope-
lessly stuck. Feeling helpless or hopeless can lead to paralysis,
and you are less likely to devote the time and effort necessary
to improve your life.[156]

Learning about research by Stanford psychologist Carol
Dweck may be the antidote you need to defy the potential dam-
age of repeated failure.[157] Dweck's studies distinguish between
a fixed mindset and a growth mindset. A person with a fixed
mindset believes that ability is by and large innate and that
meaningful change is therefore not possible. For example, I am
either good at math or not—either born with a knack for num-

bers or not. In contrast, a person with a growth mindset believes that ability can be developed and that real change is possible. For example, while I may be more or less gifted with numbers, my ability is largely variable and depends primarily on how much I invest in mathematics.

A person with a growth mindset believes that ability can be developed and that real change is possible.

Dweck's research convincingly demonstrates that a fixed mindset stifles learning and growing and keeps us stuck in our current predicament.[158] Conversely, adopting a growth mindset frees the latent potential within us, our relationships, and our organizations. How do you shift from a fixed to a growth mindset? One way is through familiarizing yourself with some of the research on *neuroplasticity*.[159]

Neuroplasticity

Until fairly recently, conventional wisdom among neuroscientists was that the brain remains fixed for most of our life. The prevailing belief was that our genetic makeup and our very early experiences determine our brain structure. Under this framework, since we had no control over our genes or the environment we inhabited during the first few years of our life, we were forced to accept the ways of our brains and to make the most of our fixed neural lot.

It was only toward the end of the twentieth century that scientists began to challenge the notion of a fixed brain. Groundbreaking research by Marian Diamond, Richard Davidson, Jeffrey Schwartz, and others demonstrated that the brain changes throughout our life, whether we are two years old or ninety-two years young.[160] In fact, through our thoughts and our actions, by choosing what we focus on and what we do, we can control how and when our brain changes. Neuroplasticity is the term scientists employ to describe the brain's ability to morph—to form new connections, rewire, grow, and reorganize neural networks. And it turns out that merely knowing about neuroplasticity can liberate us from the shackles of hopelessness and helplessness and empower us to embark on a change journey of our own.

> *Neuroplasticity is the term scientists employ to describe the brain's ability to morph—to form new connections, rewire, grow, and reorganize neural networks.*

One of the first studies to demonstrate neuroplasticity focused on the brains of individuals preparing for the London taxi license exam. Research by Irish neuroscientist Eleanor Maguire demonstrated that the aspiring cabbies' hippocampal structure changed following the hours, days, and months they spent memorizing the complex map of London.[161] New neural pathways emerged and old ones were reinforced, and like muscles, brain structures grew bigger and more robust. Other experiments involving professional musicians showed neuroplasticity in a different area of the brain when the musicians played and replayed a piece of music.[162] Meditating daily, even if only for a few minutes, generates significant change in the neural structure of the brain.[163] Physical exercise, interestingly, not only leads to the brain being more plastic and malleable but also stimulates *neurogenesis*—the creation of new brain cells.[164]

Merely learning about neuroplasticity, about the brain's ability to change, is often sufficient to produce the shift from a fixed to a growth mindset.[165] This mindset shift increases the likelihood that actual change will take place, because beliefs, whether paralyzing or empowering, become self-fulfilling prophecies. While a general awareness

> *Merely learning about neuroplasticity, about the brain's ability to change, is often sufficient to produce the shift from a fixed to a growth mindset.*

of the brain's malleability is a good start, a valuable milestone on the path of change, a deeper understanding of the way our brain works can take us further. Specifically, learning about the formation and transformation of neural pathways can help us appreciate the value of the 3 Rs process as well as guide us in how to best incorporate the MVIs into our life.

How Neural Pathways Are Formed

The brain comprises an intricate web of connections among the neurons, forming millions and millions of pathways of varying length and breadth. Each experience—whether brushing your teeth, memorizing a map, playing a musical instrument, or meditating—follows a particular pathway, a pattern, amid the web of neurons. What's interesting and important about the trip along the neural pathway is that the experience is not a passive traveler. Instead, the experience actively reinforces the pathway, expands and thickens it with each passing. Every time you engage in an activity—studying a map or a language, playing the piano, or hitting a tennis ball—the neural pathway associated with the activity is reinforced. As the neural pathway is reinforced, as it expands and thickens, the thought or action associated with it establishes itself deeper as second nature and is further internalized as a habit.[166] When this happens, the taxi driver can easily recall the location of a street, the musician can play a piece of music by heart, the meditator can remain calm in the midst of chaos, and the tennis player can automatically respond to a ball moving at a hundred miles per hour.

Neural pathways are formed in an analogous manner to the way streams and rivers are created in nature. As water persistently passes through a shallow and narrow channel, that

Neural pathways are formed in an analogous manner to the way streams and rivers are created in nature.

channel gradually widens and deepens. Some of the largest rivers started off as little streams and grew bigger over time with the natural reinforcement of flowing water. A one-time rush of water, even if extremely powerful, is unlikely to create a major channel. A great deal of water over a long period of time needs to flow over the same area to break ground.

In the same way that a one-off rush of water is insufficient to form a channel, a single epiphany or a rarely repeated action is unlikely to create a major neural pathway. For a neural pathway to expand and thicken—for habits and rituals to form—repetition is essential.

Once a neural pathway is formed, it functions as a self-reinforcing system. The implication of this is that new information coming in is more likely to flow through an already-established neural pathway than to create a new one. Going back to our analogy, water is more likely to flow through an established, existing channel than it is to flow along a new or random pattern on the ground. Once a neural pathway is formed, more information is able to pass through it, expanding it further and making it more likely that future information will flow through the pathway, which will then further expand and thicken it. The self-reinforcing system means that thoughts and behaviors are likely to follow the path of their predecessors, further reinforcing the path, making it even more likely that new thoughts and behaviors will follow the same path.[167]

Helpful and Harmful Neural Pathways

Neural pathways can be beneficial or detrimental, healthy or unhealthy, empowering or disempowering, helpful or hurtful.[168] For someone with a strong tendency toward anxiety, the neural pathways associated with worry are broad and well established, like the earth's most ancient rivers. A passing comment from a colleague that for most people would virtually go unnoticed could generate serious angst in a chronically anxious individual. For this individual, the neural pathways associated with anxiety are well established and attract information coming from the outside into their midst—just like well-established rivers attract water coming from the outside. As more anxiety is experienced by the individual, the neural pathway is further reinforced, making it even more likely that future experiences will follow the same pathway and compound the anxiety. A person who easily gets angry is likely to have wide neural pathways in the part of the brain associated with aggression. Each time this person gets angry, sometimes at the slightest provocation, it creates a downward spiral by further reinforcing the existing tendency to fly off the handle.

In contrast, in the brain of a person with a cheerful outlook or a calm disposition, the neural pathways associated with these pleasurable states are thick. External events or internal thoughts are more likely to gravitate toward these established pathways and to be experienced by the person as pleasurable. These pleasant experiences create an upward spiral, further reinforcing the existing cheerful and calm disposition, making future pleasant events more likely.

How you react in any given situation is, to some extent, a function of the thickness of your particular neural pathways. Taken together, these pathways determine your "general disposition." What is important to keep in mind, though, is that even though this general disposition may be deeply rooted—after being reinforced for an extended period of time—you can still decide to alter it by modifying your neural pathways. Recognizing the malleability of the brain is the foundation of a growth mindset.

The 3 Rs and Neuroplasticity

The 3 Rs can and do change neural pathways. Repeating a sentence over and over again—whether it's about accepting emotions, acting with integrity, leading a healthy lifestyle, or slowing down—reinforces that particular way of thinking and being. Repeating the gratitude exercise reinforces a healthy pathway and over time produces a more positive outlook on life as a whole. Gradually, you can sculpt your brain, shape it, and draw closer to the best version of yourself.[169]

The 3 Rs can and do change neural pathways.

Understanding how our brains work explains why repetition is an essential part of the change process. Reminding ourselves once or twice or even ten times about something, no matter how important it is to us, is usually insufficient to produce enduring impact. One of the most famous and successful taglines in advertising history is Nike's "Just Do It!" It makes perfect sense that advertising executives would craft the pithiest and most memorable line to represent the brand. If those advertising executives had happened to be behavioral psychologists—and thankfully they were not—they might have landed on a much clunkier, much less lucrative, but more accurate tag line: "Just do it, and then do it again, and again, and again." This is the only reliable path to lasting change.

Just do it, and then do it again, and again, and again.

12

Action Plan

> As I accumulated dozens of new habits—mostly
> tiny ones—they combined to create a transfor-
> mation. Sustaining all this did not feel hard.
> Pursuing change in this way felt natural and
> oddly fun.
>
> —B. J. Fogg[170]

The list of twenty MVIs that I present in this book is neither exhaustive nor complete. There are numerous additional happy habits that you can incorporate in your daily life—some may be variations on those that I suggested, whereas others may be entirely different. Your first step is to list the happy habits you wish to implement, or at least experiment with, in your life. Your list may include some of the MVIs in this book, either precisely as I describe them or modified to suit your needs, as well as additional happy habits that you generate beyond those I offer.

As you may recall, I derived the term MVI from the term MVP (Minimum Viable Product). The purpose of MVPs is for companies to collect feedback and gain experience—so they can improve the next version of the product that comes out. It's similar with MVIs. Through feedback and experience, you can improve on a particular intervention so that over time it better fits your specific needs and wants.

Create a Personal Plan

Your next step after generating your list of MVIs is to create a written weekly plan for introducing these happy habits into your life. Your plan, in all likelihood, will not include all the MVIs—that would be too much—so pick and choose the ones that are most appealing and relevant to you at a given time. For example, you may decide that finding more meaning at work is a priority for you now, and a few months from now you may focus more on changing perspective. Moreover, not all happy habits in this book are right for you, while there are doubtless ones that have not found their way into this book that may be just what you need. After you come up with a plan, keep in mind that it's bound to change over time as you evolve and as your environment changes. Be attentive to your particular needs and to the effects of the interventions on you.

Be attentive to your particular needs and to the effects of the interventions on you.

As I mentioned previously, the plan has to be aligned with your personal routine. For example, if you're already physically active in the afternoon, introducing high-intensity bursts of exercise may make sense in the morning but not later in the day. The same redundancy may apply if your office or home has stairs that you regularly climb up and down, though you may decide to throw in a few upper-body exercise bursts. If you're doing yoga regularly, stretching or meditation may not be an essential part of your plan, and if you're an avid reader, engaging with quotes and excerpts may not add that much value. And if hugs are an integral part of your life, it may not be necessary to explicitly commit to additional ones—though hugging is one of those things that you can never overdose on.

Three Typical Days

I would like to share with you three typical days of a person who works a nine-to-six office job and has little time or inclination to go to the gym or attend yoga classes with any regularity. While the plan for each of the three days is unique, there are similarities among them. In addition to the daily plan, this person has incorporated two additional reminders. The first is a bracelet she wears as a reminder to engage in informal meditation, reminding herself to return to the here and now in whatever she may be doing. The second is a picture on her desk of her loving grandmother as a reminder to bring more hugs and other forms of touch back into her life.

As you look through the example below, you may feel overwhelmed by the amount of daily MVIs. Remember the discussion around the butterfly effect—less may be more when it comes to implementation. And while you can choose to include as many as fifteen of the happy habits from this book in your life, you can also choose to incorporate just one or two of them. As long as they become rituals, you will reap significant benefits. Small changes make a big difference when consistently applied.

Small changes make a big difference when consistently applied.

The VIVID App: Creating Your Daily Plan

You can follow the instructions in VIVID to create your own daily plan. Remember to make the plan fit your particular needs, which you can do by slightly modifying one of those I designed or by creating a new one that is entirely different.

If you haven't yet scanned a QR code in this book, you can scan the one below.

DAY 1

07:00 AM	Start the day with one minute of *formal meditation*, focusing on the breath going in and out. Come up with a couple of *appreciative questions* to guide you through the day.
07:15 AM	Following a warm shower, spend a minute taking a *cold shower.*
08:45 AM	Do *jumping jacks* for thirty seconds. Don't overexert yourself. It's still early in the day!
10:15 AM	Run up the office stairs for at least thirty seconds. If more opportunities to do so arise throughout the day, grab them!
11:45 AM	Run on the spot with your knees up for thirty seconds. Then spend one minute in a forward bend, focusing on the gentle stretch in your hamstrings.
01:15 PM	Do push-ups for thirty seconds or longer with your arms wide apart. Spend one minute standing up straight, arms clasped behind your back, gently stretching your chest and shoulders while focusing on the physical sensation.

02:45 PM	Run up the office *stairs* for at least thirty seconds. Slowly and deliberately *read* an Emily Dickinson poem.
04:15 PM	Hold yourself in a plank position for thirty seconds or longer. Then, for a total of ninety seconds (forty-five on each side), lie down in a spinal twist, where one leg is straight and the other bent and then crossed over the straight leg. Focus on the sensation in your back.
05:45 PM	Think of a difficult experience you had today or previously, and then shift your perspective so you can see the positive in it. Finally, take in three gentle, slow, and deep breaths.
07:15 PM	Skip rope for thirty seconds or longer.
09:15 PM	With weights in both hands, do ten to fifteen *squats*, slowly descending and then ascending. Then stretch your quadriceps by standing on one leg and grabbing the other foot with the opposite hand. Switch sides, stretching the other quad muscle.
10:00 PM	Before going to bed, spend a minute or two giving yourself permission to be human by observing whatever emotion is present in your mind and your body Then, take a minute to write down and visualize at least five things for which you are grateful.

DAY 2

07:00 AM	Start the day with one minute of formal meditation, focusing on the breath going in and out. Take two minutes to journal about anything that is on your mind, be it something that makes you happy or something that is bringing you down.
07:15 AM	Following a warm shower, spend a minute taking a cold shower.
08:45 AM	Lunge forward on alternate legs for at least thirty seconds. Do not overexert yourself, given that it's still early in the day.
10:15 AM	Run up the office stairs for at least thirty seconds. If more opportunities to do so arise throughout the day, grab them!
11:45 AM	Skip on one leg and then on the other for a total of at least thirty seconds.
01:15 PM	Hold a *plank* for thirty seconds or longer. Then spend one minute standing up, looking up with arms stretched straight up and back, gently opening your chest and shoulders while focusing on the physical sensation.
02:45 PM	Run up the office *stairs* for at least thirty seconds. Slowly and deliberately, *read* your favorite quote of the day.
04:15 PM	Lying on your back, for thirty seconds or longer, bring your head, neck, and upper back up while *cycling* your feet off the ground. For a total of ninety seconds (forty-five on each side), lie down on the floor with one leg straight and the other clasped to your chest. Focus on the sensations in your legs.

05:45 PM	Come up with an idea for a *relationship booster* and commit to making it happen.
07:15 PM	*Dance* for a minute or so, moving your legs and arms. Then sit against the wall, bringing the soles of your feet together while pushing your legs down with your elbows for a gentle groin stretch. Focus on the breath going in and out.
09:15 PM	With weights tied to your ankles, lie on your belly and slowly bend your knees, bringing your heels to your buttocks and then slowly back to the floor. Following the *strengthening* exercise, *stretch* your hamstrings by extending your legs as you sit in a forward bend position.
10:00 PM	Before going to bed, take a minute to write down and visualize at least five things for which you are *grateful*. Then engage in one or two minutes of four-seven-eight breathing.

DAY 3

07:00 AM	Start the day with one minute of *formal meditation*, focusing on the breath going in and out. For two minutes, write about what you are already doing that is *meaningful* to you.
07:15 AM	Following a warm shower, spend a minute taking a *cold shower.*
08:45 AM	*Jump* on the spot for thirty seconds, allowing your arms to move about freely. Do not overexert yourself.
10:15 AM	Run up the office *stairs* for at least thirty seconds. If more opportunities to do so arise throughout the day, grab them!

11:45 AM	*Run* on the spot for at least thirty seconds, bringing your feet to your buttocks.
01:15 PM	Do *push-ups* for thirty seconds or longer with arms parallel to shoulders. Then, while standing up, for 30 seconds twist your back to one side and look behind you, then do the same in the other direction.
02:45 PM	Run up the office *stairs* for at least thirty seconds. Slowly and deliberately *read* a book excerpt that you love.
04:15 PM	Assume a *plank* position for 30 seconds while raising one foot from the floor. Then switch to the other foot for 30 seconds. For 30 seconds or longer, lie down and peel your buttocks and back off the floor to create a *bridge* with your body. Focus on the sensations in your body.
05:45 PM	Reflect on kind acts that you've committed over the past week, and commit to at least five extra *acts of kindness* for the coming week.
07:15 PM	Do *pull-ups* and then gently extend your elbows as you *stretch* your biceps.
9:15 PM	Hold the *lunge* position until your muscles burn. *Stretch* by sitting on your shins, stretching the fronts of your feet, and resting your groin on your calves. Focus on the breath going in and out.
10:00 PM	Before going to bed, take a minute to write down and visualize at least five things for which you are *grateful*. Take a minute for slow, deep breathing—inhale slowly and gently through your nose and all the way down to your belly, and then slowly exhale through your nose as your belly drops.

Take Action, Now!

Peter Drucker is considered by many to be the father of modern management studies. He was born in 1909 and died in 2005, a week short of his 96th birthday. Throughout his life Drucker traveled the world, speaking to thousands and thousands of managers and leaders. In his later years, however, he preferred not to travel much, so instead of venturing out to speak to people, he had people come to him. Fortune 500 CEOs, political leaders, senior executive groups—they all flocked to Claremont, California, to spend a magical weekend with the grandmaster of management.

The way Drucker started off these weekends was by telling participants that on Monday, when they went back to their "real" life, to their homes and offices, he didn't want them to call him up and rave about the amazing time they had. Rather, he wanted them to tell him what new behaviors they were introducing. He would say: "On Monday, don't tell me how great it was; tell me what you're doing differently."[171]

Why? Because after spending more than sixty years in the business of change, Peter Drucker understood that most change efforts fail, that an insight following a weekend retreat or a self-help book, no matter how great, usually brings about nothing more than the honeymoon effect. It doesn't matter how powerful a learning experience is, most people go back to where they were before the experience. Those who do enjoy lasting change don't rest on their laurels and revel in their insight, but instead do things differently immediately following the experience. In his book *The Effective Executive* Drucker

It doesn't matter how powerful a learning experience is, most people go back to where they were before the experience.

describes how a new practice becomes a habit, how we turn a new idea into an embedded ritual: "Practices can always be learned . . . They have to be acquired, as we all learn the multiplication table; that is, repeated ad nauseam until '6 times 6 is 36' has become unthinking, conditioned reflex, and firmly ingrained habit. Practices one learns by practicing and practicing and practicing again."[172]

Transform Your Life!

The idea underlying this book—that small interventions consistently applied can make a big difference—has great potential to transform your life. Each of the interventions covered in this book can potentially make a real difference in your day-to-day. However, no matter how deep your understanding of the content of this book, no matter how much it resonates with you, change can only come about by taking action.

Change can only come about by taking action.

So which MVIs are you going to introduce into your life? Which reminders are you going to set up, which actions are you going to engage in repeatedly, and which rituals are you going to cultivate? Starting today, what are you going to do differently?

APPENDIX A

The VIVID App

Over the years, the more I understood the depth of the knowing-doing gap, the more I became interested in finding ways to bridge it. We read books, attend lectures, even feel deeply moved or inspired. But then, life happens. We forget. We postpone. We fall back into familiar patterns. The insight remains, but the change we hoped for doesn't materialize. The biggest challenge in personal growth isn't acquiring knowledge—it's applying it.

I felt there must be a better, more effective way to support people in bringing about lasting, meaningful change. I envisioned a world where personal growth experts could not only provide their audience with information but also help them with transformation. Toward that end, I founded VIVID—a social impact start-up aimed at bridging the knowing-doing gap through evidence-based, interactive practices.

Grounded in neuroscience, behavioral psychology, and research on habit formation, VIVID AI's platform allows experts around the world to design and deliver structured, personalized practice plans that turn insight into action. VIVID offers support mechanisms including:

➤ A ready-made practice plan, so you can begin without having to design the structure yourself
➤ Tools to adjust the plan to your own rhythm and needs
➤ Options to involve friends or professionals for encouragement and accountability
➤ Simple ways to track your progress and reflect on your experience and growth
➤ Gamification of your experience to make it fun and effective
➤ Continuous improvements to help you persist and bring about lasting change.

The VIVID platform has already been used by experts around the world, providing the infrastructure for lasting change to individuals seeking personal development to global organizations looking to boost employee wellbeing.

To learn more about VIVID or explore practice plans, visit the QR codes provided throughout the book or go to www.vivid .me. The tools are ready. The plan is waiting. The next step is yours.

APPENDIX B

Lee Albert's Magnificent Seven ©

The Magnificent Seven muscle-balancing movements are designed to effectively address the most common muscle imbalances that can lead to pain. By holding each stretch for at least one minute, you can promote healing and improve your overall wellbeing. Choose the option for each pose that feels best for you; these stretches can be performed in any order. Embrace these transformative stretches for a stronger, more balanced body.

Stretch Wrist Flexors

Instructions:

-Stand or sit up straight.
-With open palms, slowly bring your hands together.
-Gently push your palms together.
-Keep your fingers spread.
-Gently squeeze your shoulder blades together.
-Feel a stretch on the palm side of your wrists and in the fingers.

Benefits:

-Balances muscles of the hand and forearm.
-Helps with hand, wrist and elbow discomfort.
-Helps Carpal Tunnel.
-Helps Arthritis in the hand and fingers.

Stretch Quads

Instructions:

-Slowly ease yourself into position so you are sitting on your heels
-If this is painful, place pillows or blankets under your buttocks
-If this is still painful, practice one of the other versions until
your quads loosen a bit.
-Feel a stretch on the front side of your thigh
-Feel a stretch in your chest

Benefits:

-Balances muscles on the front and back of the thigh
-Helps with low back pain
-Helps with knee pain
-Promotes better posture

Option 1

Option 2

Stretch Chest

Instructions:

-*Stand up straight.*
-*Face palms forward.*
-*Keep your fingers spread.*
-*Gently squeeze your shoulder blades together.*
-*Do not lock your knees.*
-*Feel a stretch in the chest.*

Benefits:

-Balances muscles of the upper back and chest.
-Balances muscles of the hand and forearm.
-Helps with hand, wrist and elbow discomfort.
-Leads to better posture and less overall pain.
-Helps with shoulder and neck pain.
-Helps with back pain.

Strengthen Backside of the Body

Instructions:

-Lying on your back, place your feet flat on the floor.
-Arms at your side with the palms facing down.
-Press the back of your shoulders, your feet and palms into the floor and lift your hips up.
-Clasp hands and squeeze shoulder blades together.

Benefits:

-Balances muscles of the front and back of the body.
-Strengthens the back of the body.
-Stretches the front of the body.
-Helps with back, hip and knee pain.

Option 1

Tip: If this movement hurts your neck or is too difficult, skip for now until your body is more balanced.

Stretch Calves

Instructions:

-*From a standing position, place hands on the floor.*
-*Keep knees bent.*
-*Press heels toward the floor.*
-*Feel a stretch in the calves.*

Benefits:

-Helps with foot, ankle and knee pain.
-Increases circulation.
-Relieves back pain.
-Helps with plantar fasciitis.

Option 1

Stretch Psoas

Instructions:

-*Stand up straight, feet hip width apart.*
-*Bring the left foot forward about 2-3 feet.*
-*Keep the back leg straight and press the heel of that leg into the floor.*
-*Do not lock your knees.*
-*Bring arms out to the side, spread fingers, squeeze shoulder blades.*
-*Feel a stretch in the chest, calf and front of the thigh.*
-*Repeat on the other side.*

Benefits:

-Balances muscles of the upper back and chest.
-Balances muscles of the hand and forearm.
-Helps with hand, wrist and elbow discomfort.
-Balances muscles of the lower leg.
-Helps with back, hip and knee pain.

Option 1

Option 2

Stretch Outside Thigh & Piriformis

Instructions:

-Sit upright on the floor or bed with your legs extended.
-Cross your left leg over and place your foot next to your right thigh.
-Reach your left arm behind you and place your hand on the floor.
-Use your right arm to pull the leg into a stretch.
-Feel a stretch on the outside thigh and the buttocks.
-Repeat on the other side.

Benefits:

-Balances muscles of the outer & inner thigh.
-Balances muscles of the hand and forearm.
-Balances muscles of the hip.
-Helps with back, hip and knee pain.

Option 1

Tip: If this stretch is too deep, place foot on the inside of the thigh instead of the outside.

Option 2

APPENDIX C

Additional Reading

Following is a list of books that provide a deeper understanding of the MVI concept as well as actual bite-sized interventions that you can easily implement in your life.

Amabile, T., & Kramer, S. (2011). *The Progress Principle: Using Small Wins to Ignite Joy, Engagement, and Creativity at Work*. Harvard Business Review Press.

Bartlett, J., & O'Brien, G. (Ed.). (2022). *Bartlett's Familiar Quotations*. Little, Brown.

Baumeister, R. F., & Tierney, J. (2012). *Willpower: Rediscovering the Greatest Human Strength*. Penguin Books.

Clear, J. (2018). *Atomic Habits: An Easy & Proven Way to Build Good Habits & Break Bad Ones*. Avery.

Duhigg, C. (2014). *The Power of Habit: Why We Do What We Do in Life and Business*. Random House.

Fogg, B. J. (2021). *Tiny Habits: The Small Changes That Change Everything*. Harvest.

Hardy, D. (2022). *The Compound Effect: Jumpstart Your Income, Your Life, Your Success.* John Murray One.

Johnson, B. (2023). *Areté: Activate Your Heroic Potential.* Heroic Blackstone.

Maurer, R. (2014). *One Small Step Can Change Your Life: The Kaizen Way.* Workman.

Olson, J. (2013). *The Slight Edge: Turning Simple Disciplines Into Massive Success and Happiness.* Greenleaf Book Group Press.

Pessin, A. (2009). *The 60-Second Philosopher: Expand Your Mind on a Minute or So a Day!* Oneworld.

Thornton, M. (2006). *Meditation in a New York Minute: Super Calm for the Super Busy.* Sounds True.

Wiseman, R. (2010). *59 Seconds: Change Your Life in Under a Minute.* Anchor.

ENDNOTES

For the sake of convenience, throughout this book I will use the terms MVIs and *happy habits* interchangeably.

We of course also inherit part of our psychological makeup from our physical constitution. Genes, for instance, affect our psychological state.

REFERENCES

1. Ben-Shahar, T. (2007). *Happier: Learn the secrets to daily joy and lasting fulfillment.* McGraw Hill.
2. Ben-Shahar, T. (2009). *The pursuit of perfect: How to stop chasing perfection and start living a richer, happier, life.* McGraw Hill.
3. Marrow, A. (1969). *The practical theorist.* Knopf.
4. Kingsolver, B. (2023). *Small wonder: Essays.* Harper Perennial.
5. Ries, E. (2011). *The lean startup: How today's entrepreneurs use continuous innovation to create radically successful businesses.* Crown Currency.
6. Proctor, C. (Ed.). (2017). *Positive psychology interventions in practice.* Springer.
7. Ockham, W. (1990). *Philosophical writings* (P. Boehner, Ed. & Trans.). Hackett.
8. Frederick, S. (2007). Hedonic treadmill. In Baumeister, R. F. and Vohs, K. D. (eds.). *Encyclopedia of Social Psychology.* Sage.
9. Thaler, R. H., & Sunstein, C. R. (2021). *Nudge: The final edition.* Penguin Books; Fogg, B. J. (2021). *Tiny habits: The small changes that change everything.* Harvest.
10. Yoshida, R., Murakami, Y., Kasahara, K., Sato, S., Nosaka, K., & Nakamura, M. (2024). Minimum intensity of daily six eccentric contractions to increase muscle strength

and size. *Scandinavian Journal of Medicine & Science in Sports*, 34(6), Article e14683.

11.   Buettner, D. (2012). *The Blue Zones: 9 lessons for living longer from the people who've lived the longest*. National Geographic.

12.   Drive Research Team. (2024). *New Year's resolution statistics and trends*. Drive Research. https://www.driveresearch.com/market-research-company-blog/new-years-resolutions-statistics

13.   Langer, E. J. (1989). *Mindfulness*. Addison-Wesley.

14.   Thorp, J. (2024, March 20). Gen Z: A return to orthodoxy [Blog post]. *Beyond Sunday*. https://jeffmthorp.substack.com/p/gen-z-a-return-to-orthodoxy?utm_campaign=post&utm_medium=web

15.   Baldwin, C. (2007). *Storycatcher: Making sense of our lives through the power and practice of story*. New World Library.

16.   Emmons, R. (2008). *Thanks! How practicing gratitude can make you happier*. HarperOne.

17.   Hatfield, E., Cacioppo, J. T., & Rapson, R. (1993). *Emotional contagion*. Cambridge University Press.

18.   Robinson, J. (2025). *Learn from Oprah: 5 life-changing gratitude quotes you need to hear*. https://www.josierobinson.com/journal/oprahgratitude

19.   Kesavayuth, D., Binh Tran, D., & Zikos, V. (2022). Locus of control and subjective well-being: Panel evidence from Australia. *PLoS One*.

20.   Imai, M. (1986). *Kaizen: The key to Japan's competitive success*. McGraw Hill.

21.   Carter, C. (2020). The 1-minute secret to forming a new habit [Video]. TED Conferences. https://www.ted.com/talks/christine_carter_the_1_minute_secret_to_forming_a_new_habit/transcript

22.   Yan, B., & Zhang, X. (2022). What research has been conducted on procrastination? Evidence from a systematical bibliometric analysis. *Frontiers in Psychology*.

23.   Cuddy, A. (2018). *Presence: Bringing your boldest self to your biggest challenge*. Little, Brown.

24. Pychyl, T. A., & Flett, G. L. (2012). Procrastination and self-regulation failure: An overview of the theoretical, research, and treatment literature. *Cognitive and Behavioral Practice.*

25. Robbins, M. (2021). *The high-5 habit: Take control of your life with one simple habit.* Hay House.

26. Dizikes, P. (2011). When the butterfly effect took flight. *MIT News Magazine.*

27. Loehr, J., & Schwartz, T. (2004). *The power of full engagement: Managing energy, not time, is the key to high performance and personal time.* Free Press.

28. Kimball, C. E. (1988). *The writings of Camilla Eyring Kimball.* Deseret Book.

29. Aristotle. (1954). *The Nicomachean ethics* (D. Ross, Trans.). Oxford University Press.

30. Keller, H. (1903). *Optimism: An essay.* T. Y. Crowell.

31. Dalai Lama. (2009). *The art of happiness: A handbook for living.* Riverhead Books.

32. Ben-Shahar, T. (2021). *Happiness studies: An introduction.* Palgrave Macmillan.

33. Ben-Shahar, T. (2021). *Happier, no matter what: Cultivating hope, resilience, and purpose in hard times.* The Experiment.

34. Santi, J. (2021). *17 one-minute habits that will change your life.* The EveryGirl. https://theeverygirl.com/one-minute -habits-that-will-change-your-life

35. Rana, D. (2023). *Everyday 1-minute habits that are guaranteed to level up your life in 6 months.* Medium. https:// medium.com/publishous/everyday-1-minute-habits-that -are-guaranteed-to-level-up-your-life-in-6-months -e303420a82fd

36. Eliot, G. (2007). *Janet's repentance.* Hesperus Press.

37. Frankl, V. (2006). *Man's search for meaning.* Beacon Press.

38. Wrzesniewski, A., & Dutton, J. E. (2001). Crafting a job: revisioning employees as active crafters of their work. *Academy of Management Review.*

39. Ibid.

40. Buckingham, M., & Clifton, D. (1996). *Now, discover your strengths*. Putnam Adult.

41. Peterson, C., & Seligman, M. E. P. (2004). *Character strengths and virtues: A handbook and classification*. Oxford University Press.

42. Drucker, P. (2001). *The essential Drucker*. Harper Business.

43. Ben-Shahar, T., & Ridgway, A. (2017). *The joy of leadership: How positive psychology can maximize your impact (and make you happier) in a challenging world*. Wiley.

44. Ibid.

45. Hanh, T. N. (2008). *The miracle of mindfulness: The classic guide*. Rider & Co.

46. Christopoulou, E., & Pavlopoulos, V. (2025). A review on meditation: History, transcendental dimensions and application. *Psychology and Psychotherapy*.

47. Guthrie, C. (2008). Mind over matter through meditation. *O: The Oprah Magazine*. https://www.oprah.com/health/a-3-minute-dose-of-meditation

48. Blankert, T., & Hamstra, M. R. W. (2016). Imagining success: Multiple achievement goals and the effectiveness of imagery. *Basic and Applied Social Psychology*.

49. Baer, D. (2020). Use LeBron James' simple visualization ritual to get what you want out of the new year. *Business Insider*. https://www.businessinsider.com/forget-resolutions-use-lebron-james-visualization-ritual-for-success

50. Daly, A. (2017). What's actually the difference between mindfulness and meditation? *Women's Health*. https://www.womenshealthmag.com/life/a19941792/mindfulness-vs-meditation

51. Hanh, T. N. (2008). *The miracle of mindfulness: The classic guide*. Rider & Co.

52. Obama, M. (2013). First Lady Michelle Obama on the health of women and their families [Blog post]. *Let's Move*. https://letsmove.obamawhitehouse.archives.gov/blog/2013/05/14/first-lady-michelle-obama-health-women-and-their-families

53. Lathia, N., Sandstrom, G. M., Mascolo, C., & Rentfrow, P. J. (2017). Happier people live more active lives: Using smartphones to link happiness and physical activity. *PLoS One*.

54. Ratey, J. J. (2013). *Spark: The revolutionary new science of exercise and the brain*. Little, Brown.

55. Shetty, M. (2023). The benefits of HIIT and other forms of interval training. *Stanford: Lifestyle Medicine*. https://longevity.stanford.edu/lifestyle/2023/09/05/the-benefits-of-hiit-and-other-forms-of-interval-training

56. Atakan, M. M., Li, Y., Koşar, Ş. N., Turnagöl, H. H., & Yan, X. (2021). Evidence-based effects of high-intensity interval training on exercise capacity and health: A review with historical perspective. *International Journal of Environmental Research and Public Health*.

57. Ho, B. H., Lim, I., Tian, R., Tan, F., & Aziz, A. R. (2018). Effects of a novel exercise training protocol of Wingate-based sprint bouts dispersed over a day on selected cardiometabolic health markers in sedentary females: A pilot study. *BMJ Open Sport and Exercise Medicine*.

58. WHO Media Team. (2024). *Nearly 1.8 billion adults at risk of disease from not doing enough physical activity*. World Health Organization. https://www.who.int/news/item/26-06-2024-nearly-1.8-billion-adults-at-risk-of-disease-from-not-doing-enough-physical-activity

59. Lurati, A. R. (2018). Health issues and injury risks associated with prolonged sitting and sedentary lifestyles. *Workplace Health and Safety*.

60. Albert, L. (2018). *Live pain-free: Eliminate chronic pain without drugs or surgery*. Dudley Court Press.

61. Albert, L. (2023). *Live pain free: All natural, drug free pain relief*. https://www.leealbert.com

62. Nall, R. (2024). Are there any health benefits to a cold shower? *Medical News Today*. https://www.medicalnewstoday.com/articles/325725#boosted-mood

63. Beard, A. (2018). Cold showers lead to fewer sick days. *Harvard Business Review*.

64. Hame, S. L. (2023). *6 cold shower benefits to consider.* UCLA Health. https://www.uclahealth.org/news/article/6 -cold-shower-benefits-consider

65. Cleveland Clinic. (2024). *The benefits and risks of cold plunges.* https://health.clevelandclinic.org/what-to-know -about-cold-plunges

66. Nestor, J. (2020). *Breath: The new science of a lost art.* Riverhead Books.

67. Benson, H. (2000). *The relaxation response.* William Morrow.

68. Brown, R. P., & Gerbarg, P. L. (2012). *The healing power of the breath: Simple techniques to reduce stress and anxiety, enhance concentration, and balance your emotions.* Shambhala.

69. Weil, A. (2013). *Spontaneous happiness: A new path to emotional well-being.* Little, Brown Spark.

70. Huberman Lab. (2023). Breathwork protocols for health, focus & stress. *Neural Network Newsletter.* https://www .hubermanlab.com/newsletter/breathwork-protocols-for -health-focus-stress

71. Young, M. (2022). How and why to try alternate nostril breathing. *Cleveland Clinic: Health Essentials.*

72. Lancar, T. (2021). A decade of power posing: Where do we stand? *The Psychologist.* https://www.bps.org.uk /psychologist/decade-power-posing-where-do-we-stand

73. Disraeli, I. (2005). *Curiosities of literature.* Project Gutenberg. https://www.gutenberg.org/cache/epub/16350/pg16350-images .html#AN_ENGLISH_ACADEMY_OF_LITERATURE

74. Newberg, A., & Waldman, M. R. (2013). *Words can change your brain: 12 conversation strategies to build trust, resolve conflict, and increase intimacy.* Avery.

75. Ibid.

76. Easwaran, E. (2016). *Passage meditation: A complete spiritual practice.* Nilgiri Press.

77. Orem, S. L., Binkert, J., & Clancy, A. L. (2007). *Appreciative coaching: A positive process for change.* Jossey-Bass.

78. Cooperrider, D. L., & Whitney, D. (2005). *Appreciative inquiry: A positive revolution in change.* Berrett-Koehler.

79. Goldsmith, M., & Reiter, M. (2015). *Triggers: Creating behavior that lasts: Becoming the person you want to be.* Crown Currency.

80. Cooperrider, D. L., & Whitney, D. (2005). *Appreciative inquiry: A positive revolution in change.* Berrett-Koehler.

81. Horney, K. *Self-analysis.* W. W. Norton.

82. Pennebaker, J. W. (1997). *Opening up: The healing power of expressing emotions.* Guilford Press.

83. Burton, C. M., & King, L. A. (2003). The health benefits of writing about intensely positive experiences. *Journal of Research in Personality.*

84. Burton, C. M., & King, L. A. (2007). Effects of (very) brief writing on health: The two-minute miracle. *British Journal of Health Psychology.*

85. Campbell, E. (2015). Six surprising benefits of curiosity. *Greater Good Magazine.* https://greatergood.berkeley.edu /article/item/six_surprising_benefits_of_curiosity

86. Swan, G. E., & Carmelli, D. (1996). Curiosity and mortality in aging adults: A 5-year follow-up of the Western Collaborative Group Study. *Psychology and Aging.*

87. Suzuki, S. (2020). *Zen mind, beginner's mind: Informal talks on Zen meditation and practice.* Shambhala.

88. Langer, E. J. (1989). *Mindfulness.* Addison-Wesley.

89. Langer, E. J. (2010). *Counterclockwise: A proven way to think yourself younger and healthier.* Hodder.

90. Mabie, H. W., Hale, E. E., & Forbush, W. B. (2006). *Childhood's favorites and fairy stories.* Project Gutenberg. https://www.gutenberg.org/files/19993/19993-h/19993-h .htm

91. Waldinger, R., & Schulz, M. (2025). *The good life: Lessons from the world's longest study on happiness.* Rider & Co.

92. Gottman, J. M., & Silver, N. (2015). *The seven principles for making marriage work: A practical guide from the country's foremost relationship expert.* Harmony.

93. Twain, M. (1906). Letter to Gertrude Natkin. In *Mark Twain quotations, newspaper collections, & related resources.* http://www.twainquotes.com/Compliment.html

94. Bernstein, T. (2021). *12 hugs a day.* Greenwich Pediatric Associates. https://greenwichpediatrics.com/12-hugs-a-day

95. Lyubomirsky, S. (2008). *The how of happiness: A scientific approach to getting the life you want.* New York: Penguin Press.

96. Dueren, A. L., Vafeiadou, A., Edgar, C., & Banissy, M. J. (2021). The influence of duration, arm crossing style, gender, and emotional closeness on hugging behaviour. *Acta Psychologica.*

97. Field, T. (2003). *Touch.* Bradford Books.

98. Heatley Tejada, A., Dunbar, R. I. M., & Montero, M. (2020). Physical contact and loneliness: Being touched reduces perceptions of loneliness. *Adaptive Human Behavior and Physiology.*

99. Field, T. (2003). *Touch.* Bradford Books.

100. Dunn, E. W., Aknin, L. B., & Norton, M. I. (2008). Spending money on others promotes happiness. *Science.*

101. Lyubomirsky, S. (2008). *The how of happiness: A scientific approach to getting the life you want.* New York: Penguin Press.

102. Frank, A., & Frank, O. (1997). *The diary of a young girl.* Bantam.

103. Goleman, D. (2004). *Destructive emotions: How can we overcome them?* Bantam.

104. Kawamichi, H., Yoshihara, K., Sasaki, A. T., Sugawara, S. K., Tanabe, H. C., Shinohara, R., Sugisawa, Y., Tokutake, K., Mochizuki, Y., Anme, T., & Sadato, N. (2014). Perceiving active listening activates the reward system and improves the impression of relevant experiences. *Social Neuroscience*; Kluger, A. N., & Bouskila-Yam, O. (2018). Facilitating listening scale. In D. L. Worthington & G. D. Bodie (Eds.), *The sourcebook of listening research.* Wiley.

105. Schwartz, D. (2020). Just listening to kids can do wonders for their self-esteem. *Psychology Today*. https://www .psychologytoday.com/us/blog/adolescents-explained /202004/just-listening-to-kids-can-do-wonders-for-their-self -esteem

106. Kluger, A. N., & Itzchakov, G. (2022). The power of listening at work. *Annual Review of Organizational Psychology and Organizational Behavior*.

107. Shafir, R. Z. (2003). *The Zen of listening: Mindful communication in the age of distraction*. Quest Books.

108. Ibid.

109. Hutson, R. (2024). *Reflections on Fred Rogers' healing power of presence*. Fred Rogers Institute. https://www .fredrogersinstitute.org/resources/reflections-on-fred-rogers -healing-power-of-presence

110. Keller, H. (1996). *The story of my life*. Dover.

111. Ben-Shahar, T. (2010). *Being happy: You don't have to be perfect to lead a richer, happier life*. McGraw Hill.

112. Williams, M., Teasdale, J., Segal, Z., & Kabat-Zinn, J. (2024). *The mindful way through depression: Freeing yourself from chronic unhappiness*. Guilford Press.

113. Rabbit-Duck Illusion. (1892). *Fliegende Blätter*.

114. Tomaka, J., Blascovich, J., Kibler, J., & Ernst, J. M. (1997). Cognitive and physiological antecedents of threat and challenge appraisal. *Journal of Personality and Social Psychology*.

115. Flusberg, S. J., Holmes, K. J., Thibodeau, P. H., Nabi, R. L., & Matlock, T. (2024). The psychology of framing: How everyday language shapes the way we think, feel, and act. *Psychological Science in the Public Interest*.

116. Brooks, A. W. (2014). Get excited: Reappraising pre-performance anxiety as excitement. *Journal of Experimental Psychology: General*.

117. Wrzesniewski, A., & Dutton, J. E. (2001). Crafting a job: Revisioning employees as active crafters of their work. *Academy of Management Review*.

118. Edmondson, A. C. (2023). *Framing failure for learning and innovation.* HBS Executive Education. https://www.exed .hbs.edu/blog/framing-failure-for-learning-innovation

119. Schnarch, D. (1998). *Passionate marriage: Keeping love and intimacy alive in committed relationships.* Owl Books.

120. Eliot, G. (1998). *Middlemarch.* Wordsworth.

121. Cicero, M. T. (1913). *On duties* (W. Miller, Trans.). Harvard University Press.

122. Emmons, R. A., & McCullough, M. E. (2003). Counting blessings versus burdens: An experimental investigation of gratitude and subjective well-being in daily life. *Journal of Personality and Social Psychology.*

123. Lyubomirsky, S. (2008). *The how of happiness: A scientific approach to getting the life you want.* Penguin Press.

124. Emmons, R. (2008). *Thanks! How practicing gratitude can make you happier.* HarperOne.

125. Fredrickson, B. L. (2001). The role of positive emotions in positive psychology: The broaden-and-build theory of positive emotions. *American Psychologist.*

126. Branden, N. (1971). *The psychology of self-esteem.* Bantam Books.

127. Omoogun, A. (2019). *This is what you should aim for instead of rushing through life.* Medium. https://medium.com/mind -cafe/this-is-what-you-should-aim-for-instead-of-rushing -through-life-846c72cafeb5

128. Johnson, C. D. (2012). *Memory, metaphor, and Aby Warburg's atlas of images.* Cornell University Press.

129. Clear, J. (2018). *Atomic habits: An easy & proven way to build good habits & break bad ones.* Avery.

130. Plato. (1997). *Complete works* (J. M. Cooper, Ed.). Hackett.

131. Thaler, R. H., & Sunstein, C. R. (2021). *Nudge: The final edition.* Penguin Books.

132. De Botton, A. (2013). *Religion for atheists: A non-believer's guide to the uses of religion.* Vintage.

133. Doidge, N. (2007). *The brain that changes itself: Stories of personal triumph from the frontiers of brain science.* Penguin Life.

134. Ibid.
135. Durant, W. (2022). *The story of philosophy*. Dover.
136. Easwaran, E. (2016). *Passage meditation: A complete spiritual practice*. Nilgiri Press.
137. Rosenthal, R., & Jacobson, L. (2003). *Pygmalion in the classroom: Teacher expectation and pupils' intellectual development*. Crown House.
138. Collins, M. (1992). *Ordinary children, extraordinary teachers*. Hampton Roads.
139. Carden, L., & Wood, W. (2018). Habit formation and change. *Current Opinion in Behavioral Science*.
140. Wood, W., & Runger, D. (2016). Psychology of habit. *Annual Review of Psychology*.
141. Langbridge, F. (2023). *The happiest half hour: Sunday talks with children*. Legare Street Press.
142. Ben-Shahar, T. (2014). *Choose the life you want: The mindful way to happiness*. The Experiment.
143. Goleman, D., Boyatzis, R., & McKee, A. (2013). *Primal leadership: Unleashing the power of emotional intelligence*. Harvard Business Review Press.
144. James, W. (2018). *The principles of psychology*. Project Gutenberg. https://www.gutenberg.org/files/57628/57628 -h/57628-h.htm
145. Aristotle. (1954). *The Nicomachean ethics* (D. Ross, Trans.). Oxford University Press.
146. Kahneman, D. (2013). *Thinking, fast and slow*. Farrar, Straus and Giroux.
147. Hume, D. (1985). *A treatise of human nature*. Penguin Books.
148. Mendelsohn, A. I. (2019). Creatures of habit: The neuroscience of habit and purposeful behavior. *Biological Psychiatry*.
149. Bacon, F. (2000). *The new organon*. Cambridge University Press.
150. Kahneman, D. (2013). *Thinking, fast and slow*. Farrar, Straus and Giroux.
151. Ricard, M. (2010). *Why meditate? Working with thoughts and emotions*. Hay House.

152.   Amabile, T. M., & Kramer, S. J. (2011). The power of small wins. *Harvard Business Review.*

153.   Schwartz, J. M., & Gladding, R. (2012). *You are not your brain: The 4-step solution for changing bad habits, ending unhealthy thinking, and taking control of your life.* Avery.

154.   Chaiton, M., Diemert, L., Cohen, J. E., Bondy, S. J., Selby, P., Philipneri, A., & Schwartz, R. (2016). Estimating the number of quit attempts it takes to quit smoking successfully in a longitudinal cohort of smokers. *BMJ Open.* Edmondson, A. C. (2023). Framing failure for learning and innovation [Blog post]. *HBS Executive Education.* https://www.exed.hbs.edu/blog/framing-failure-for-learning-innovation

155.   Forleo, M. (2015). How to be consistent: 5 steps to get things done, all the time [Blog post]. *Marie Forleo Blog.* https://www.marieforleo.com/blog/be-consistent

156.   Scherer, K. R. (2022). Learned helplessness revisited: Biased evaluation of goals and action potential are major risk factors for emotional disturbance. *Cognition and Emotion.*

157.   Dweck, C. (2005). *Mindset: The new psychology of success.* Ballantine Books.

158.   Yeager, D. S., & Dweck, C. S. (2020). What can be learned from growth mindset controversies? *American Psychologist.*

159.   Sarrasin, J. B., Nenciovici, L., Foisy, L. B., Allaire-Duquette, G., Riopel, M., & Masson, S. (2018). Effects of teaching the concept of neuroplasticity to induce a growth mindset on motivation, achievement, and brain activity: A meta-analysis. *Trends in Neuroscience and Education.*

160.   Costandi, M. (2016). *Neuroplasticity.* MIT Press.

161.   Maguire, E. A., Woollett, K., & Spiers, H. J. (2006). London taxi drivers and bus drivers: A structural MRI and neuropsychological analysis. *Hippocampus.*

162.   Olszewska, A. M., Gaca, M., Herman, A. M., Jednoróg, K., & Marchewka, A. (2021). How musical training shapes

the adult brain: Predispositions and neuroplasticity. *Frontiers in Neuroscience.*

163. Goleman, D., & Davidson, R. J. (2018). *Altered traits: Science reveals how meditation changes your mind, brain, and body.* Avery.

164. Ben-Zeev, T., Shoenfeld, Y., & Hoffman, J. R. (2022). The effect of exercise on neurogenesis in the brain. *Israel Medical Association Journal.*

165. Sarrasin, J. B., Nenciovici, L., Foisy, L. B., Allaire-Duquette, G., Riopel, M., & Masson, S. (2018). Effects of teaching the concept of neuroplasticity to induce a growth mindset on motivation, achievement, and brain activity: A meta-analysis. *Trends in Neuroscience and Education.*

166. Costandi, M. (2016). *Neuroplasticity.* MIT Press.

167. Dresp-Langley, B. (2020). Seven properties of self-organization in the human brain. *Big Data and Cognitive Computing.*

168. Kuznecova, T. (2024). *How neuroplasticity can help to alleviate anxiety.* Centric Mental Health. https://www.mentalhealth.ie/mental-health-wellness-blog/how-neuroplasticity-can-help-to-alleviate-anxiety

169. Cohen, G. L., & Sherman, D. K. (2014). The psychology of change: Self-affirmation and social psychological intervention. *Annual Review of Psychology.*

170. Fogg, B. J. (2021). *Tiny habits: The small changes that change everything.* Harvest.

171. Wartzman, R. (2010). Drucker's question: What will you do differently on Monday? *Harvard Business Review.*

172. Drucker, P. F. (2006). *The effective executive: The definitive guide to getting the right things done.* Harper Business.

ACKNOWLEDGMENTS

Expressing gratitude is one of those activities that require—and deserve—much more than a minute or a page. No amount of time and space would be enough to truly thank the people in my life who make my work possible and who, in particular, have made this book possible. Still, I'd like to try.

Without the unwavering support and thoughtful feedforward of Ashley Michael, this book would not have seen the light of day. I am grateful to my literary agent Paula Munier who believed in this book from the outset and refused to give up on it—or on me.

I am deeply grateful to Centenary University. The very first time I set foot on Centenary's campus, I knew I had arrived at my academic home—a rare and beautiful place where ambition is grounded in humbleness, passion is guided by wisdom, and the pursuit of happiness is a shared endeavor.

CJ Lonoff's kindness and generosity are contagious and inspire me to continue to spread goodness. I find it hard to imagine where I would be today without her presence in my life.

I have learned and continue to learn from Gidi Kadosh, Almog Cohen, Noam Shwartz, and Be'er Twito—my partners at VIVID. They are making our world a better place, one day at a time.

To the dream team at Alcove Press—Laura Apperson, Stephanie Manova, Rebecca Nelson, Thaisheemarie Fantauzzi Pérez, and Melissa Rechter—thank you for your care, wisdom, and belief in this project. Working with you has been a gift, and I hope it's the beginning of a beautiful friendship.

My family is my anchor, my fuel, my motivation, and my inspiration. My mom and dad are the best role models I could have asked for in life. I am forever grateful for Tami's MVIs— kind words and words of wisdom a plenty, loving smiles, and warm heartfelt hugs strewn throughout the day—all of which add up to a lifetime of bliss. David, Shirelle, and Eliav never cease to amaze me and fill my days with joy and meaning. My siblings and their families bring light and love to my life and to the world.

I'm dedicating this book to my fellow journeyers—colleagues, students, and friends from the Happiness Studies Academy. Together, minute by minute, we are bringing about the happiness revolution.

INDEX